# GROW YOUR OWN TEA

# GROW YOUR OWN TEA

## THE COMPLETE GUIDE TO
## Cultivating, Harvesting, *and* Preparing

**CHRISTINE PARKS AND
SUSAN M. WALCOTT**

Timber Press
Portland, Oregon

Photo and illustration credits appear on page 198.

Published in 2020 by Timber Press, Inc.

The Haseltine Building
133 S.W. Second Avenue, Suite 450
Portland, Oregon 97204-3527

timberpress.com

Printed in China on paper from responsible sources

Second printing 2022

Text design by William van Roden

Cover design by Kim Thwaits

ISBN 978-1-60469-931-9

Catalog records for this book are available from the Library of Congress and the British Library.

This Camellia Forest tea with flowers is ready to infuse.

# CONTENTS

# Preface

THE IDEA FOR THIS BOOK came to us on a beautiful sunny summer day in Oregon. Susan and I were on a trip to Minto Island Tea Company, driving through the flat agricultural land of the Willamette Valley to visit their gardens. While sharing our excitement over the growing number of farmers across the United States making homegrown tea, we envisioned writing a short guide for tea lovers and gardeners, to document this living history as it unfolds and encourage local tea tourism. Most people have no idea that tea can grow, has been grown, and is currently being grown in North America, the British Isles, and other locations outside Asia. Many people are surprised to learn that the tea plant is a kind of camellia and can be grown wherever ornamental camellias grow. Furthermore, despite a bounty of information available to members of the global tea industry about how to grow and make tea on a commercial scale, limited resources have been available to guide new and small-scale tea growers. As Susan and I arrived at our destination and met with Elizabeth Miller at Minto, we enthusiastically agreed that more people should know about homegrown tea.

My own family has grown tea for decades, as one of the hundreds of types of camellias in our North Carolina collection at Camellia Forest. We made tea to drink, following a simple recipe for sun drying. In the early 2000s, after visiting Hangzhou, home of the famous Dragon Well (or Longjing) tea, the China National Tea Museum, and amazing tea gardens, I became seriously hooked on tea and dove headfirst into studying and cultivating it. Humbled by its deep history around the world, I soon realized I could spend the rest of my life learning about tea and never run out of questions.

My husband, David, and I planted a species and test garden with hundreds of tea plants on a hillside near our home. We sought out and consulted other small tea farms across the United States, sharing practical experiences and lessons learned through avid research. When I attended the Atlanta World Tea Expo in 2007, I felt like quite the anomaly—a US tea grower. As I walked through the crowds, I was stunned by the diversity and enthusiasm of vendors and tea fanciers. Since then, my passion for all things tea has deepened. I became a leader in tea at the American Camellia Society, holding tea education seminars and workshops and taking every opportunity to introduce people to the possibilities of homegrown, handmade tea.

Susan's journey with US-grown tea began at a grocery store in Indiana, where she was intrigued by the eye-catching label for American Classic tea, produced by Charleston Tea Plantation. Her first academic job at Atlanta's Georgia State University was close enough to Wadmalaw Island, where the tea is produced, that she was able to visit and tour the plantation. She was even lucky enough to buy a tree descended from Lipton's earliest US tea endeavors in the 1880s.

A geographer whose curiosity about origins led to an exploration of the many worlds of tea, Susan has traveled extensively for research. She too visited Hangzhou, where she tried Dragon Well tea and high-mountain strains. She also sampled a variety grown in the jungle that is pressed into cakes for export then served with salt and a dollop of yak butter. She has visited tea gardens across Hawaii and traced Lipton's search for suitable US tea-growing sites as an alternative to those in China during the turbulent Cultural Revolution of the mid-1960s and 1970s. Happily, Susan also came to work at the University of North Carolina in Greensboro, where the small world of local tea brought us together.

This tale of tea aficionados is not unusual, among a community of friendly, enthusiastic growers. Many home gardeners grow tea for its health benefits, for the simple pleasures of gardening, and for the satisfaction of creating a fresh, handcrafted brew. Tea is generally a passion first—one that sometimes grows into a business. In recent years, Camellia Forest's tea garden has more than tripled in size. We now make more than enough tea to drink and share with friends and customers, which is my greatest reward.

As with any relationship, growing your own tea is a commitment that thrives on work as well as fun. An increasing interest in local and sustainable food systems, and awareness of tea as a healthy artisan beverage, has inspired new tea growers of all types to get started. As a result, tea farms are popping up across diverse regions in nontraditional tea-growing countries. Susan and I are grateful for the opportunity to share what we've learned along our journeys so far, and we invite you to join us in our adventure.

Welcome to tea time!

# Introduction

*Tea is quiet and our thirst for tea is never far from our craving for beauty.*

JAMES NORWOOD PRATT

Pots and cups from China, Thailand, and the United Kingdom illustrate the global appeal of tea.

ONE OF THE MOST widely shared claims about tea is that, after water, it's the second most popular beverage in the world. Yet, despite tea's popularity, few people outside major tea-growing regions are aware of how it is grown and processed. Most people don't even realize that all the different kinds of tea we enjoy come from just one species of the beautiful flowering camellia. That doesn't stop us from loving it though, this camellia in our cup.

An increased interest in local production and sustainability, as well as the health benefits and artisan qualities of tea, is leading to an increased smallholder trend in the United States and other areas outside of traditional tea-growing regions. Although much tea is grown and produced at a large commercial scale, it's estimated that 70 percent of tea around the world is grown by individuals, everywhere from family backyards to plots surrounding village communities. While working on this book we surveyed dozens of small-scale commercial tea farmers and over one hundred private tea gardeners to narrow down what aspiring tea growers want and need to know. Almost 80 percent of our respondents grew between one and ten tea plants, most growing directly in the garden, but some in pots. A majority of private growers (62 percent) admitted that they've never harvested their plants—many because they don't know how and others because their plant simply never flourished. Of those who had not yet made tea, most said it was due to a shortage of leaves. Almost half declared their biggest challenge was lack of knowledge, followed by coping with weather extremes. Over 80 percent use their crop to make green tea. Most make the tea for themselves, while a few growers have turned their tea into commercial endeavors. The vast majority came to tea growing because they simply love to drink tea and love the idea that they can grow their own.

Our focus here is on these gardeners and small-scale farmers who want to learn how to cultivate their own homegrown, handmade tea. Types of cultivated tea and the flavors of the brewed cup come in infinite varieties, reflecting the plants' terroir, as shaped by climate, type of soil, amount of sun, and surrounding plants and insects. Climate, especially, impacts the chemistry of the leaf both at harvest and during processing. With knowledge and ingenuity, growers have a world of possibility for cultivating and making their own teas.

The healthy green leaves of a tea plant.

To help you find *your* place in the history of tea production, we'll start out by looking at tea's historic roots, then jump forward in time to sample regions of contemporary production in North America and the British Isles. Then we take a deep dive into the nature of the tea plant itself, so you become equipped with an understanding of its versatile and fascinating qualities.

The bulk of the book provides a step-by-step map for successfully navigating your own journey from root to refreshing cup of tea. Along the way, we've gathered stories from companion tea growers whose experiences can teach (or console) you, and summaries of the most important lessons we've learned. We'll address how to choose a plant (and how to propagate your own); where to plant for best results based on your soil, sun, and climate; and how to maintain and harvest your leaves. Once your plant is growing and healthy, we'll discuss how to make the different types of tea, from the least processed white, to green, oolong, and black. We include ideas for gardening with tea and a few other ways to use this remarkable plant. We also heartily encourage tea tourism, either virtual or in person, to learn more about tea and to support fellow growers nearby or around the world.

# TYPES OF TEA FROM A TO Z

This is a primer on some basic teas. There are infinite names for versions of the four main teas made from *Camellia sinensis* (black, oolong, green, and white), with regional and producer distinctions that range from smoking to adding other elements for flavor. Many teas include the name of the location where they originate, a description of what the leaves look like (eyebrows, gunpowder, needles), or a distinguishing addition (flowers). We discuss processing for many of these teas; others are beyond the scope of home growers, but are good to know about.

| TYPE | ORIGIN OR HISTORY | PROCESSING | CHARACTERISTICS |
|------|-------------------|------------|-----------------|
| ASSAM | A high-elevation state of India with big-leaf trees | A black tea from large Indian tea plant leaves | Light, earthy flavor |
| BLACK | Mostly from southern China | Highly oxidized (exposed to air, so leaves turn a dark color) | Strong, brisk flavor |
| CHAI | An Indian name for tea with spices | Black tea, often with ginger, cinnamon, pepper, sugar, cardamom, boiled milk | A spicy-sweet milky mix |
| DARJEELING | From the West Bengal state of India near Tibet | A small-leaf, black, Indian-type tea | Aromatic, flavorful black tea |

| TYPE | ORIGIN OR HISTORY | PROCESSING | CHARACTERISTICS |
|------|-------------------|------------|-----------------|
| GREEN | Almost 80% of commercial green tea is produced in China's southern provinces | Oxidation is less than for black or oolong and is prevented by heat and drying | Green color, light flavor; many varieties, some grassy |
| GUNPOWDER | Chinese green or oolong tea leaves rolled to preserve flavor; originated in China's Tang Dynasty | Single tea leaves are tightly rolled into small pearls or pellets | Flavorful; preserves well; opens slowly in boiled water |
| JASMINE | Black or green tea, usually not top quality, so enhanced by additive | Tea with jasmine flowers added for flavor or scent | Floral, like jasmine |
| LONGJING (DRAGON WELL) | Chinese green tea from eponymous village in Hangzhou | Green tea pan-fire roasted soon after picking to halt oxidation | Long, flat, slender leaves; premium quality |
| MATCHA | Originated in China, popularized in Japan | Dried green tea is ground into a powder, then whisked until frothy | Bright green, grassy flavor |
| NUWARA ELIYA | Famous Ceylon (Sri Lanka) tea grown since British introduction in 1867 | Classic, very high quality black/red and green teas on mid-island, high-elevation estates | Delicate and fragrant, with notes of cypress, mint, and eucalyptus |

# TYPES OF TEA *continued*

| TYPE | ORIGIN OR HISTORY | PROCESSING | CHARACTERISTICS |
|------|-------------------|------------|-----------------|
| **OOLONG** | A classic Chinese tea | Mature leaves (usually three plus bud); elaborate processing, including sun withering and varying degrees of controlled oxidation | Between lighter green and darker black teas; sophisticated flavors |
| **PU'ERH** | Named for trading town in the southwestern province of Yunnan during China's Tang Dynasty; discovered after tea fermented during travel | Harvested from very old, large-leaf trees; pressed into cakes; traditional "raw, wild" variety is slow-aged; some new varieties are "cooked" to hurry the process | Earthy, dark flavor; highest quality improves with age (some varieties are aged for decades) |
| **RED** | Chinese term for black tea, referring to color of the brew when steeped | Same as black tea | Same as black tea |
| **SENCHA** | Japanese green tea in which the whole leaf is infused but not ground and included in the drink, as with matcha; most popular tea in Japan | Generally grown in full sun; first flush can contain stems, small shoots; steamed after harvest | Sophisticated to rough, depending on leaf quality |
| **WHITE** | Named for the Chinese word referring to bud color | Made from buds; most lightly processed tea variety | Delicate, light flavor and color |

| TYPE | ORIGIN OR HISTORY | PROCESSING | CHARACTERISTICS |
|---|---|---|---|
| YELLOW | Usually made with leaves from China's Hunan Province | Produced similar to green tea with special step of covering leaves with a cloth to steam slightly while warm for slow, light oxidation | Mellow flavor, distinct yellow color |
| ZHU YE QING (GREEN BAMBOO TEA) | From southwest Sichuan Province mountains; named in 1964 by China's foreign minister, Chen Yi, who said the taste reminded him of bamboo shoots | Green tea with long, slender, first-flush leaves, pressed to dry in a hot wok | Slightly vegetal; needle shaped, the leaves float upright when steeped, which could also have contributed to the name |

Tea flowers alongside their ornamental cousins. When the delicate white blooms appear in autumn, they remind us that tea is a type of camellia.

# A WORLD OF TEA

# A Brief History of Tea

*The things that people cannot do without every day are firewood, rice, oil, salt, soybean sauce, vinegar, and tea.*

WU TZU-MU

According to legend, almost 5,000 years ago a leaf fell into Chinese emperor Shen Nung's cup of simple boiled water, blown down from the shady tree under which he was meditating. The resulting drink kept him alert and awake—features that still appeal to modern tea drinkers. The first writings about tea come from Chinese sage Lu Yu, who wrote *Tea Classic* (*Ch'a Ching*) around 780 CE. Using poetic language, he described the basics of producing and consuming an already very popular drink. Tea drinking soon spread from meditating monks to nobles and wealthy elites. Implements for storing, serving, and sipping showcased the sophistication of their owners—objects so artistic, we display them in museums today. Chinese teas range from the least processed (white teas) to the darkest (black teas). A subject of international intrigue and commerce, tea represented the refined civilization of its Middle Kingdom homeland.

The tea plant, *Camellia sinensis*, and its related species probably originated in the upland border triangle of Myanmar, northeastern India (the state of Assam), and southwestern China's province of Yunnan. Yunnan villages were historically the beginning of the Tea Horse Road. Dried tea pressed into circles and square bricks, sometimes stamped with designs, was piled high in baskets carried by men and horses.

**WINDING THROUGH REMOTE** areas of the high Himalayas, their route led to market destinations in Tibet and India. Word of the wakefulness-promoting drink spread throughout Asia. Japanese monks adopted tea in the ninth century. By the twelfth century, Japanese feudal elites also enjoyed the drink—they created schools for preparing and serving tea and supported the artists making utensils to prepare and drink it. Green teas developed during this time, such as powdered *matcha* and rolled *sencha*, and varieties roasted with grains, such as *genmaicha*, remain popular in Japan today. Seventh-century Korean Buddhists drank tea, as did Mongolians exposed to cosmopolitan culture when they ruled China during the Yuan Dynasty.

Tea around the world owes its name to local Chinese dialects. Tea for Europe left from ports in South China and was called *te* in the local dialect. Tea going to Russia and India left from North China where it was called *cha*. A drink made from this *cha* became *chai* with the addition of Indian spices such as black pepper, cardamom, ginger, and cinnamon.

Porters with stacks of pu'erh brick tea bound for Tibet along the Tea Horse Road circa 1908.

# Tea Travels West

**AS THE FIRST EUROPEANS** to round Africa's Cape of Good Hope, Portuguese explorers brought word of the tea beverage back from their trips into China. British society picked up the tea habit in the seventeenth century. A leading London newspaper in the mid-1600s commented with amazement that the hard-drinking Scots had even given up their breakfast whisky in favor of tea! The fondness of British residents for tea as a stimulating antidote to their region's prevailing damp, chilly weather is well documented over several centuries, but supplying Britain with its favorite drink throughout history has been far from simple.

For decades, the British drank tea from China because China was the only place that produced tea. This created a trade deficit, in which imperial China had something the British Empire wanted but the Brits had nothing of equal value to exchange for it. That is until the British East India Company realized they could trade for tea with an even more addictive plant: the opium poppy. Britain cultivated opium in India, but prohibited consumption there because its dangerous addictive effects were well known. Instead, they grew it primarily as a means to trade for tea. When China pushed back against the plague

Illustration of a Chinese tea plantation from Fortune's 1853 book, *Two Visits to the Tea Countries of China and the British Tea Plantations in the Himalaya*.

of imported opium, it sparked what we know today as the Opium Wars, which again threatened Britain's supply of tea. The British needed an alternative tea source.

But growing tea outside of China was no simple matter. The tea plant became a target of international espionage. The aptly named Robert Fortune, an early nineteenth-century Scottish botanist and plant hunter, first secured plants from China with the intention of growing them in British colonial India. The plants, and the workers who knew how to process them, were taken out of China illegally— if caught, the penalty for turning over state secrets would have been death. It was difficult to preserve delicate cuttings from existing plants during the long sea and overland trip to India so they'd survive to be planted on British-owned soil. To top it all off, tea wasn't actually drunk by most Indians at the time, so the British needed to get locals hooked on the brew to increase the local market.

In addition to the Chinese plants, British traders began cultivating a variation of tea discovered growing in India's hilly Assam Province. This variation, along with the stolen Chinese varieties planted in Darjeeling, eventually resulted in a robust tea supply that kept Brits in the cuppas to which they'd become accustomed. England's relationship with its American and Indian colonies was heavily influenced by attempts to control the lucrative tea trade.

Modern-day Fujian Province looks much the same as when Robert Fortune snuck into China to learn about tea.

# The North American Experience

**DESPITE THE EARLY** colonists' reputation for rejecting tea—the Boston Tea Party was their reaction to Britain's attempts to control the cost of tea during the trade deficit with China—the brew remained popular in North America.

*Camellia sinensis* was in popular demand during colonial times. In 1799, French botanist André Michaux was the first to plant tea in North America, at his Charleston-area Middleton Barony plantation. Rich agricultural regions growing rice and indigo in South Carolina and Georgia were the first locations in the future United States for *Camellia sinensis*–based tea cultivation. These areas were a natural fit for growing tea, as their coastal plain soils feature a tea-friendly combination of thick sand, clay, marl, and calcium carbonate combined with a fine, sandy loam. Generally sunny weather and mild temperatures also favored cultivation. However, irregular rainfall was a challenge that growers didn't solve until the mid-twentieth century.

In 1828, William Prince, of the Linnaean Botanic Garden in Flushing, New York, was supplying green and bohea tea plants for cultivation in South Carolina's humid climate. Junius Smith's Golden Grove Plantation in Greenville, South Carolina, was one of the largest antebellum tea-growing locations in the nation. Smith relied on plants imported from India. In his 1848 collection of essays and lectures, Smith enthusiastically proclaimed that he was "sanguine in the belief that the cultivation of the Tea Plant in the United States will open a brilliant career to practical husbandry. . . . Exempt from the bondage of intellectual servitude, to which the people of China, from the earliest ages of their national existence, have been subject, the American husbandman comes fresh and unshackled by antiquated oriental notions, to the free choice and adoption of such improvements in the culture and preparation of Tea as his own unrestrained, unbiased, and cultivated intellect may prescribe." Despite Smith's success at Golden Grove, and his arrogant faith in the superiority of American tea growers over their Chinese counterparts, his plantation died with him when he was shot in 1853.

Sharing Smith's optimism, the US government distributed free seeds and plants throughout the mid- to late 1800s to encourage growing tea throughout the Southeast to promote agricultural self-sufficiency. But lack of efficient transportation connecting the agricultural South and major domestic markets in the North depressed the market for southern products such as tea. Labor costs were another stumbling block for US-based tea production. In sum, it was less expensive for tea buyers in Chicago, for example, to buy tea from China than to get it from Charleston. However, several planters continued to try their hand at large-scale southern plantations. Notable examples include a Dr. Jones of Liberty County, Georgia, in the 1850s, and a Dr. Forster of Georgetown, South Carolina, from 1874

Despite the Boston Tea Party, tea remained popular in the colonies, even if it never became as culturally significant as it was in Britain.

THE DESTRUCTION OF TEA AT BOSTON HARBOR.

to 1879. William Le Duc, US commissioner of agriculture under President Hayes, joined the patriotic effort to promote backyard cultivation of tea by distributing seeds throughout the South. Although the seedlings grew in a variety of locations, as they do today, the program ended under a less-enthusiastic bureaucrat.

By 1888, plant biologist Charles Shepard was growing tea plants from India, China, and Japan on his Pinehurst Tea Plantation, a former rice plantation in Summerville, South Carolina. Shepard's idea for solving the labor-cost problem combined free morning schooling for local children of recently freed slaves in exchange for afternoon work in the tea fields. The US Department of Agriculture supplied machinery, and Shepard added mule-pulled ploughs. Although the business died with Shepard in 1915, the windblown crosses of Assam hybrids, Chinese big-leaf varieties, cultivars from Taiwan, and Indian Darjeeling cultivars are still grown today on Wadmalaw Island's Charleston Tea Plantation.

Moving west, tea helped with the construction of the country's railroads. The greater health of nineteenth-century Chinese workers building the Central Pacific Railroad compared to their westward-bound, largely Irish immigrant counterparts was attributed in no small part to their boiling and straining of locally available water in preparing tea.

In the early 1870s, Japanese settlers at the Wakamatsu Tea and Silk Farm Colony in Placerville, California, tried their hand at tea growing in the foothills of the Sierra Nevada. Though they used stock familiar to them from home, the settlers struggled, in part due to drought (it turned out this area, near Sutter's Mill, was better at producing gold nuggets!), and the colony lasted only two years. However, offspring of these same tea plants were saved and grown over the years at various California sites, including a Japanese nursery in Oakland and a camellia nursery in Southern California. Descendants of these unnamed plants probably grow in many private gardens today. In June 2019, Wakamatsu rang in its sesquicentennial with a festival that celebrated the site's history and highlighted efforts of contemporary agriculturalists to raise tea more successfully with a combination of modern knowledge and sustainable methods.

Plenty of American locations hosted commercially successful tea cultivation experiments around the turn of the twentieth century. Hawaii was initially promising, but sugar's growing popularity and profitability eclipsed tea cultivation in the archipelago for another century. The towns of Pierce and Mackay in Texas sprouted tea fields in 1906 and 1907 respectively, but these were soon devasted by all-too-common Gulf of Mexico hurricanes.

Despite setbacks, clever American innovations in the realm of tea persisted, including Thomas Sullivan's muslin tea bags in 1903. A year later, during a steamy St. Louis summer day at the 1904 World's Fair, iced tea made its debut. Industrial-age contributions included new tea pruning and picking machinery by George Mitchell in 1911, continuing attempts to hold down labor costs relative to Asian pickers and processes. However, the US Department of Agriculture's decision to stop generating regular reports on the industry in 1912 signaled an end for the commercialization of domestically produced tea.

The next attempts at American-grown tea wouldn't come until the mid-twentieth century, when global tea corporation Lipton scouted many potential US tea-growing locations. Places where tea cultivation took place in the past were revisited and old plants secured. Lipton also set up experimental stations in areas with seemingly suitable climate conditions, and success producing other agricultural crops, around the Gulf of Mexico, Hawaii, and in fertile Pacific Northwest valleys. Although Lipton later abandoned or failed to pursue most of these locations, many became productive sites for today's individual tea entrepreneurs.

# Contemporary Tea Growing in North America and the British Isles

The diversity of tea-growing areas is reflected in the diversity of tea growers and their experiences. As we traveled across North America and the British Isles interviewing, researching, and collecting survey responses, Susan and I learned that many people growing tea are satisfied (and very happy) simply growing for their own use. Others either start out wanting to grow tea for sale or become inspired through their experience with fresh tea to share their product with the wider world—many growers we talked to didn't necessarily start growing tea with commerce in mind, but later expanded to produce tea for sale at markets and through local or online stores.

This chapter is just a sampling of the more well-established tea growers we were able to speak with or research while writing this book. It's not comprehensive today, and it can't imagine the full scope of a future tea landscape. However, we hope it will provide aspiring growers with insight into the range of possibilities they might adopt in a wide variety of physical settings.

# Eastern and Southern North America

**GROWERS IN EASTERN NORTH AMERICA** include smallholder farmers from Maryland to more northerly locations along the coast and all the way up near the Great Lakes. Areas protected by lake or terrain microclimates make northern tea growing possible. One of our customers recently shared that they are growing tea successfully (with occasional dieback in extremely cold winters) in their Philadelphia garden under the shelter of a large conifer.

The Southeast is the earliest North American tea-growing region and continues to support growing in a range of sizes from front-porch and backyard plants to the largest US commercial plantation. New growers in Mississippi, Alabama, the Carolinas, and Virginia show that these humid, warm regions are hospitable to tea growing. Irrigation may still be needed to balance out seasonal variations in rainfall in states stretching along the Gulf of Mexico as far west as Texas.

## SOUTH CAROLINA

Wadmalaw Island, twenty miles south of Charleston, has the soil and sunny warm weather suitable for tea cultivation, with sufficient rainfall and a humid climate. In the early 1960s, Lipton set up a 127-acre tea experiment station on Wadmalaw to revive the 320-plus varieties of tea plants Charles Shepard had grown at his Pinehurst plantation nearly one hundred years prior. Hires included William Hall, a tea taster with ties to Argentina who contributed his knowledge of that country's drip irrigation techniques. In 1987, Hall teamed up with agronomist and former Lipton tea station manager Mack Fleming to purchase the test station. The new team renamed their site the **Charleston Tea Plantation** and used it to test their innovative combination of a cotton and tobacco picker to trim the rows of tea bushes. The plantation eventually proved successful enough for purchase by Lipton rival Bigelow Tea Company in 2003. Bigelow has helped develop both tea production and tourism at the plantation, adding effective machinery for processing the harvest from May to October and expanding the site's hosting repertoire. The plantation is now a popular tourist destination, offering tours, education, and private events.

The iconic box of Charleston Tea Plantation's American Classic Tea.

## COMMERCIAL TEA GOES GLOBAL

The tea plant's ability to thrive across so many diverse climates explains why it has been able to expand across the globe and be successfully adopted into varied agricultural landscapes. The major contemporary tea-growing regions are mostly still in tea's homeland: China and India are the top two global producers. Other Asian countries producing tea include Sri Lanka, Japan, Vietnam, Korea, and Indonesia.

Within China, four diverse regions currently supply tea. Jiangnan, south of the Yangtze, China's longest river, produces the most tea. North of the Yangtze, Jiangbei is China's northernmost tea-producing region. Southwestern China, where tea evolved, includes Yunnan Province and other ancient production areas. And finally, the South China tea-growing region stretches in a belt across the country's southern border and includes Hainan, a semi-tropical island off the southeast coast.

India's northeastern, rainy upland region features bushes for both Assam and Darjeeling teas. And along India's southwest coast, the mitigating temperature effects of the Arabian Sea assist a second tea-producing region. Moderating ocean currents also help create tea-favorable sites along the Black Sea coast in northwest Turkey and in Sochi (formerly part of Soviet Georgia), famous for its popular, cold-resistant seeds.

Production in Kenya, the number-three global tea producer, started in highland foothills during British colonial times and continues today with a tradition of small (less than an acre) tea farms. Sri Lanka (formerly Ceylon) also grows its tea in mountainous foothills and is producer number four. South America supports large, irrigated, machine-harvested tea operations. Now popular in other cold climates, tea has been grown for over a century in the Sochi region of the Caucasus mountains.

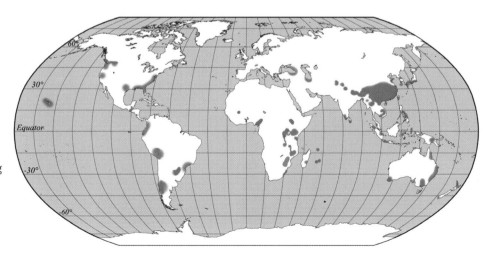

A map of traditional and commercial tea-growing areas, as well as emerging regions around the globe, illustrates the wide range of latitudes where tea is grown, spanning tropical to temperate climates.

# MISSISSIPPI

Mississippi features several aspiring tea farms. Jeff Brown and Don Vanderwerken of **JD Farms and Pearl River Tea** grow a variety of berries—principally blueberries since 2004—and, beginning in 2007, over 9,000 tea plants. Half of these come from seeds, the other half from clones. Sunny open fields nurture tea plant growth. Soil pH supports both tea and blueberries, and irrigation is only needed for the new plantings. They process their black, green, and matcha tea via machine.

**The Great Mississippi Tea Company**'s Jason McDonald started growing tea in 2013 using cultivars from the United States, Nepal, and Georgia. He presently harvests from about a quarter acre of mature plants, and adds new plants yearly, with four more acres and 20,000 plants in the field, including companion trees. In his well-equipped kitchen, he hand-processes award-winning teas, including black, oolong, and green.

In these Great Mississippi Tea Company fields, rows of new trees have been added among the young tea plants to provide future shade.

Processing equipment at Great Mississippi.

While we aren't boycotting tea or throwing it into the sea these days, it never rose to the same level of prominence in American culture as in other countries. A possible exception is iced tea, which has particular importance in the South. Iced tea is the most popular form of drinking tea in the United States, and most of the iced tea we drink comes from Argentina.

*Camellia sinensis* tea came to Argentina in the 1920s. Using seed imported from Russia and China, German immigrants pioneered successful tea cultivation in eastern Argentina's hot, humid highland region. Descendants of these farmers continue to supply a larger percentage of black tea to the United States than any other country. Argentina's high-volume tea fits the blended cut-tear-curl (CTC) quality for bags and ready-to-drink uses. Notably, mechanized tea production such as that practiced at Charleston Tea Plantation is related to Argentinian methods. Though this type of production is beyond the scope of most home growers, it is interesting to contrast the results with the whole-leaf, handmade teas we explore in this book.

## ALABAMA

Alabama's **Fairhope Tea Plantation** is close to Mobile Bay, an area that Lipton once used as a research station, and home to owner Donnie Barrett. He started with three tea plants from his father, who rescued the plants from the debris field when Lipton closed the station. Originating in sunny open fields in 1979, his cultivar *Camellia sinensis* 'Fairhope' produces primarily black and oolong teas, and now thrives at four southern universities, including in a plot at the University of Mississippi and as far afield as our tea garden at Camellia Forest in North Carolina. He estimates that some 61,000 plants currently grow at his two locations, and he has supplied seventeen other farms in the past two years. Donnie has long supported many new growers in the area by sharing his plants and knowledge.

In his own words, Barrett reports:

I process all my tea by hand, though I have a large pea sheller I sometimes use to tumble and bruise oolong and black teas. I experiment constantly with tea processing: cool before frying or put out in sun, one day in cool before drying in sun, how old, how long, on-the-ground drying or off. This will never stop. It makes me a good tea maker. Currently I pick a small batch every other weekend. I can handle it, dry it in the back of my truck in a hot parking lot, get it canned, and be ready the coming weekend to do it again. All my tea is grown in full sun—I learned this slow sun-introduction technique from the Chinese.

Weeds, I love weeds! I don't fight weeds for the first four years of tea growing. I consider tea to be a climax forest species. It will out-compete anything, especially annual weeds. At the end of the first year, after you haven't seen any tea plants for a couple months, winter kills the six-foot-tall ragweed and up pops the bright green tea. The weeds get smaller as the tea gets larger. I think tea requires this competition or does better because of it. I have large blocks of tea in the stages of tea domination that show my point.

Most of our stock has been produced from clones rooted in a cold-frame greenhouse in winter. They will spend an entire year in this greenhouse before being planted the next winter. We also have a long mature row of clones from the original Lipton plants that produces thousands of seedlings per year.

Barrett has been known to use a hedge trimmer to harvest his plants and a microwave to dry the leaves, and he occasionally diverts tourist buses from Florida to swing by for iced tea, sightseeing, and sales. With his years of experience and unique enthusiasm, Donnie is a treasured resource for the growing community of tea farmers across the South and Southeast.

## VIRGINIA

Virginia features a distinctive tea farm with roots in Korea. Since 2012, the Ramos family of **Virginia First Tea Farm** has cultivated tea plants grown from "wild tea" seeds imported from the Boseong and Hadong regions of South Korea. They're experimenting with Korean natural farming methods to cultivate their fifteen acres of bushes, which grow and flourish in full sun, mowing between the rows to efficiently manage their fields. Using only organic methods, they process black (known as red in Korea) and green tea by hand, and infuse them into probiotic castile soaps.

Fields of Virginia First Tea Farm, with Korean plants.

# Western North America

OPPOSITE Westholme Tea Company's south-facing tea field.

Western North America supports tea growing along the Pacific coast from British Columbia through California. The Pacific Northwest, including Oregon's Willamette Valley and Washington's Skagit Valley, supports a number of successful tea farms. Tea entrepreneur and former Lipton Company scout John Vendeland advises several growers in the area. He considers the verdant Willamette Valley in particular to be one of the top tea-growing locations in the country. Upon learning the potential for Northwest tea, many growers have begun new cultivation efforts—both personal and commercial. Time will tell whether this region develops into a major tea producer, as it has with wine.

## BRITISH COLUMBIA

The northernmost extent of the Pacific coast's tea cultivation is on Canada's Vancouver Island, which sits to the west of mainland British Columbia. A valley in the Cowichan region, on an eastern inlet near several area lakes, provides exceptional protection for **Westholme Tea Company**. Victor Vesely and Margit Nellemann purchased the land for this farm in 2003. Their first tea plants took root in 2010 and now number several hundred on south-facing slopes in the valley's moderate Mediterranean microclimate. As is common with large fields of its kind, picking is accomplished with help from local volunteers, who also assist in processing the garden's green, white, and oolong teas. Margit is an accomplished ceramicist and her tea-inspired vessels combined with Victor's experimental tea blends (including Canadian touches such as "maple-smoked") make for a unique visitor experience.

## OREGON

**Minto Island Tea Company**, outside Salem, Oregon, was started in 1988 by agriculturalist Rob Miller. His daughter, current co-owner Elizabeth Miller, also maintains a produce and flower farm on the site. Their oldest tea plants, established on the garden's original half-acre, are closely related to Charles Shepard's original Summerville plant collection. The garden now includes an additional nine-acre plot in a nearby field for expanded production. Oregon's dry summer months require irrigation for those fields in the open sun. They plant clover between the rows of tea—then mow it—to suppress the inevitable weeds. Picking and processing are done by hand, and the leaves are dried in a large oven.

**ABOVE** Some of Minto Island's tea plants grow in a field protected by large trees.

**RIGHT** Minto Island's production and processing manager Kacie Merkel checks on one of the large ovens Minto Island uses to dry leaves quickly.

A love of tea can lead tea shop owners to grow and process their own crop to supplement what they import from elsewhere. In 2013, Oregonian Josh Chamberlain of **J-Tea** established what he calls a "micro tea farm" around his Eugene teahouse. The Willamette Valley supports cold-weather tea cultivars, so his supply includes Sochi and Korean bushes, for a total of fifty plants. While the plants mature, the shop has been practicing—harvesting by hand and air-drying first-flush leaves on the store's counter for a simple white tea brew.

## CALIFORNIA

To the south, California's topography provides an enormous range for testing various cultivars at different elevations and with different rainfall amounts and soil conditions. For research in their extensive university system, the state of California uses seeds and cuttings from China, India, Hawaii, Taiwan, and Southern California camellia nurseries. Tea gardens and experiment stations within the University of California are currently at work on identifying tea germplasm by source. The goal is to create a network of self-supporting tea farms that would provide product and tourism experiences in coastal areas.

**Golden Feather Tea** is a great example of how tea can be grown depending on the local microclimate. Mike Fritts founded this tea garden close to Oroville, California, using tea plants sourced from old stock brought to California from Japan. Only a short drive from the hot, dry Central Valley of Northern California, his farm is situated in the foothills of rural Butte County, where the combination of silty, loamy soils, sufficient rainfall, and water for irrigation, along with low humidity and cooler temperatures, yield a high-quality leaf. Coupling hand processing with the use of a large wood-fired wok, Golden Feather produced an award-winning oolong recognized at the first US tea competition held in Hawaii in 2015. Unfortunately, severe natural disasters such as fires are all too common in today's western United States. In fall 2018, the Camp Fire damaged many plants and completely devoured buildings at Golden Feather's farm. On the bright side, some plants survived and are being tenderly cared for in hopes of a full recovery.

Tea bushes line the sides of J-Tea shop.

First-flush leaves laid out to dry on J-Tea's shop counter.

# Hawaii

**HAWAII MAY NOT HAVE** a typical North American climate, but it boasts a fascinating agricultural history, in which tea becomes a smallholder crop with a focus on artisan production. Hawaii's tea cultivation takes place across all of the main islands, from individual backyards to former sugar and pineapple plantations. Hawaiian tea production has had a roller coaster history. It began in 1887, but tea cultivation was soon eclipsed by the sugar crop. By the 1960s, given the relatively high cost of labor in the United States and transportation from Hawaii's mid–Pacific Ocean location, it was more profitable to produce sugar elsewhere, so when plantation land became available, some property went back to raising tea and coffee. Lipton surveyed the islands for tea-growing opportunities but departed before the decade was up. Kona coffee proved more successful. Coffee is easier to grow and process and has a large US market and an established brand associated with Hawaii. Currently, coffee flourishes on the west side of Hawaii's Big Island, while tea does best on the east side, but growers can be found throughout.

Tea was reintroduced to Hawaii in the late 1990s by commercial growers, but they also subsequently pulled out. Eventually, studies concluded that tea only worked as a niche product from small-scale growers. Francis Zee, a founding father of Hawaiian tea cultivation, declared that nonprofessional farmers were actually the best growers of tea. Today, however, the state of Hawaii, and several of its enterprising residents, actively support tea cultivation as a promising crop and agritourism outlet.

The University of Hawaii at Manoa's College of Tropical Agriculture and Human Resources and Hawaii's Agribusiness Development Corporation are particularly engaged in tea research. A group of state, national, and Pacific Basin organizations worked together to import tea clones selected to match Hawaiian conditions. The state's huge variety of climatic and soil conditions pose many diverse challenges. Hawaii maintains several active experimental stations (Waiakea, Mealani, and Volcano) at various elevations and with different soil mixtures. Processing is done by hand and with simple machines such as microwaves, ovens, and air-dryers.

Eva Lee, co-owner of **Tea Hawaii and Company**, has cultivated tea with her ceramic-artist and tea-grower husband, Chiu Leong, since 2002. Utilizing a forest understory, they hand-produce white, green, oolong, and black tea using traditional and imported machinery. They have also led the Hawaii Tea Society since 2004, connecting island tea growers for information exchange and helping to grow the reputation of tea grown in the state. One of their activities is bringing Asian tea experts to visit and advise about Hawaiian tea plants and processing. Tea Hawaii partners are loosely grouped as a cooperative, but vary in terms of their self-sufficiency. All are growers, but some do their own processing and marketing, while others bring their picked leaf to be processed at a shared site. Eva also gives talks and holds workshops in an effort to raise interest in tea agriculture. At present, around eight cooperative members engage in commercial production, with around fifty up-and-coming growers in various stages, some waiting for bushes to mature and some just beginning to explore planting tea.

**ABOVE** Tea pottery designed by Chiu Leong and sold at Tea Hawaii.

**LEFT** Eva Lee utilizes traditional drying racks.

# The British Isles

**IN THE NINETEENTH CENTURY,** Robert Fortune, in addition to stealing tea plants and secrets from China for British use in India, also drew up plans to explore cultivation in the home country (his efforts didn't pan out). During the Second World War, British Prime Minister Winston Churchill, well aware of the demand for tea among British workers and the military, expressed a wish for a less tenuous supply chain. However, domestic attempts to grow tea didn't flower until the early twenty-first century.

## ENGLAND

In 2005, **Tregothnan** in Cornwall pioneered the modern cultivation of tea in England on a centuries-old Boscawen family estate that has grown camellias for over 200 years. Eight miles from the coast, water and warmth create a microclimate comparable to the Himalayan foothills or North America's Pacific Northwest. The manuka tea tree, a native of New Zealand and Australia famous for its honey, also flourishes at Tregothnan and supplies some unique tea flavoring. Tregothnan tea is hand plucked and processed into classic Darjeeling and Assam black and green varieties.

## SCOTLAND

Scottish tea growers are working hard to overcome the region's climatic challenges. Chilly winter temperatures, brisk winds, heavy snow, and downpours create soggy soils and necessitate a variety of creative countermeasures such as plastic protectors, planting on sunny hillsides, and overhead coverings for early-stage plantings. The conditions also call for cold-resistant plants sourced from regions such as Nepal, Darjeeling, and Sochi. In 2015, a group of growers going by the name **Tea Gardens of Scotland** formed the Scottish Artisan Tea Producers Network. They have revived the Victorian-era practice of walled gardens and also utilize the modern practices of polytunnels and tents to protect their 40,000-plus seedlings and cuttings. A grant from the Community Food Fund (financed by the Scottish government and the European Union to support local food and drink) helped obtain the services of consultants.

Beverly Wainwright has worked in the tea industry for a decade; her latest project has been to build and run the **Scottish Tea Factory** on the edge of the Scottish Highlands. The Tea Factory provides memberships to sixteen members, including growers from the Tea Gardens of Scotland, offering processing services and tea-making classes. A small demonstration tea garden of around 700 plants was established at the factory in 2017. Windbreaks and corrugated plastic tree guards are used in winter months, when temperatures can get well below freezing, to protect the tender young plants. Beverly has also set up a community tea club to encourage locals to plant tea in their home gardens.

**Isle of Lismore Teas**, situated on the west coast of Scotland, began growing tea in October 2016. Wind is the major weather threat here—the plants are protected in tubes from November to April, and a system of low shelterbelts provides the windbreaks necessary for plants to remain uncovered the rest of the year. **Guisachan**, in the Scottish Highland village of Tomich, is the ancestral home of the golden retriever dog breed and already a popular tourist destination. The estate planted 500 tea seedlings in September 2016. In order to protect them from sun, wind, and cold, the plants are enclosed in wooden cold frames until they are established, after which they're grown in a fenced garden. Tea grows slowly this far north, but growers expect the plants to produce a fine quality leaf for making black and green tea that will enhance visitor experience.

Finally, one of the United Kingdom's most northerly tea gardens is a pilot project run by Lynne Collinson on the island of **Shapinsay in Orkney**, Scotland, launched in 2018 with an innovation grant from Highlands and Islands Enterprise. Her small backyard plot began with 1,000 Nepali cold-hardy seedlings, now sheltered under a polytunnel in raised beds.

**ABOVE** At Guisachan, tea grows protected from snow under long frames.

**OPPOSITE** Low shelterbelts protect uncovered plants at Isle of Lismore Teas.

# The Tea Plant

*In my own hands I hold a bowl of tea; I see all of nature represented in its green color. Closing my eyes, I find green mountains and pure water within my own heart. Silently sitting alone and drinking tea, I feel these become a part of me.*

SEN SOSHITSU

All major types of tea—white, green, oolong, and black—come from the leaves of *Camellia sinensis*. Early Westerners were sometimes confused as they learned about the nature of tea's botanical origins—they thought that different types of tea came from different plants. It eventually became clear that the main differences in tea types came from processing techniques and not the plant itself. However, in some ways there is truth to the initial belief, as different tea cultivars help to determine the quality of the flavors and aromas most appreciated within each type. Many varieties of *Camellia sinensis* evolved in different geographic regions and climates, and cultivars and processing methods have been developed to optimize the most distinctive characteristics of the tea we drink.

The Chinese word for camellia, *Cha Hua*, can be literally translated as "tea flower." Indeed, tea is by far the most popular camellia grown around the world. Legend has it that ornamental camellias were introduced to Western collectors by the Chinese, who, protective of their commercial interests in tea, substituted *Camellia sinensis* seeds with non-tea camellias. Imagine the surprise when the difference was discovered! Certainly, it was a disappointment to some; but what a treasure it was for the many horticulturalists and gardeners who have gone on to enjoy the diversity and impressive flower forms of *C. sasanqua* and *C. japonica*. By contrast, the tea flower is considerably less impressive, though still attractive to pollinators.

# Tea Plant Basics

**TWO VARIETIES OF** *Camellia sinensis* are considered to be "true" teas: var. *sinensis* and var. *assamica*. The first, var. *sinensis*, is the plant widely grown throughout China, the one smuggled out by the British for their own tea production. The second is named for the Assam region of India where it was "discovered" growing in the forests—whether it's native to that area is up for debate, since it has been cultivated for so long and was similar to the large-leaf tea plants grown in southern China. The general shape of leaves from both varieties is serrated and oblong, and the new growth used for tea looks remarkably similar. However, several distinctions in physical characteristics, where and how they grow, and the types of teas produced from their leaves distinguish one from the other.

*Camellia sinensis* var. *sinensis* is a multistemmed shrub, with a wide variability in leaf size, shape, and pubescence (short hairs usually seen on the new bud and underside of the leaf). It usually grows in temperate to subtropical and high-altitude tropical regions. *Camellia sinensis* var. *assamica* is more of a small tree with a single stem or trunk and is better suited to subtropical and tropical regions. While leaf size and shape vary greatly, the leaves of var. *assamica* are typically larger than var. *sinensis*, which is why the varieties are sometimes simply called "large" and "small" leaf tea. However, some varieties with var. *sinensis* origins can have leaves as large as var. *assamica*.

Unlike leaf size, tea flower characteristics are less variable. Much smaller than those of most ornamental camellias, tea flowers are between 1 inch and 1½ inches in diameter, and almost always white with six to eight petals (sometimes more) and bright yellow centers. This most vibrant feature includes 100–300 stamens (about ¼–½ inch long, topped with anthers full of pollen that are very attractive to pollinators) and a pistil made up of a style, ovary, and stigma. In var. *sinensis*, the style is fused at about half the total length before splitting into three or four arms. In var. *assamica*, the style is united for a greater part of its length before splitting. Although these may seem like small differences, they are visible without magnification (though you may need your reading glasses) and can be useful in telling apart plants with otherwise similar growth habit and leaf morphology. The differences may be even more apparent and manipulated more easily when the flowers dry out a bit after picking.

There are plenty of other differences between these two varieties. For example, var. *sinensis* sprouts new growth faster than var. *assamica*, but, in our experience, var. *assamica* plants have longer seasonal

A new leaf bud emerges, covered with a light pubescence.

New growth and a mature leaf from the two main tea varieties, var. *sinensis* and var. *assamica*, are presented here to show the leaf-size range (var. *sinensis* is the smaller sprig).

## NOMENCLATURE

Various botanical names for the tea plant have emerged over the centuries, from its initial classification as *Thea sinensis* (*sinensis* is often used in botanical names to note a plant originated in China). The most current nomenclature groups tea in the family Theaceae, genus *Camellia* L., section *Thea* (L.) Dyer. With increasing information about genetics and other characteristics of tea and related species, scientists will continue to identify and debate the differences between various types. But indisputably, the vast majority of cultivated tea plants belong to the species *Camellia sinensis*.

Tea flowers bloom in fall, sometimes while leaves are still growing, though generally growth slows dramatically by this time as the plants approach dormancy.

# TWO MAIN VARIETIES OF *CAMELLIA SINENSIS*

| | VAR. *SINENSIS* | VAR. *ASSAMICA* |
|---|---|---|
| **NATURAL FORM** | Multistemmed shrub (up to 15 feet) | Single-stemmed tree (20 feet or more) |
| **LEAF SIZE (LENGTH × WIDTH)** | 1–5 × 0.5–2 inches | 3–6 × 1–2.5 inches |
| **FLOWER MORPHOLOGY** | Fused style splits halfway up | Unified style before splitting close to the top |
| **CLIMATE/ GEOGRAPHIC REGIONS** | High-altitude tropical, subtropical, and temperate | Subtropical and tropical |
| **UNIQUE FEATURES** | Faster new growth under temperate conditions | Earlier and later growth under temperate conditions |
| **CHEMICAL DIFFERENCES** | More aromatic compounds contribute to distinctive flavor profiles in green, white, or oolong teas | More of certain catechins contribute to black tea astringency |

Leaves from two var. *assamica*-type plants at Camellia Forest highlight the incredible diversity in form despite shared genetic heritage. Though var. *assamica* tends to be sensitive to cold temperatures, both of our plants have survived decades of growth under the shelter of pine woods in our temperate North Carolina climate.

Two leaves and a bud for cocoa tea from *Camellia ptilophylla*.

growth (earlier and later). Among the many factors contributing to differences in tea flavors, var. *assamica* cultivars tend to have more of certain catechins that contribute to black tea astringency, while var. *sinensis* plants have been shown to have more of the treasured aromatic compounds enjoyed in green and oolong tea. We grow mostly var. *sinensis*, so our black teas tend to be more delicate and aromatic. I sometimes blend them with tea from the few var. *assamica* plants in our garden for a brisker cup.

## AWESOME DIVERSI-TEA

Over time, *Camellia sinensis* varieties evolved in nature and through the long history of cultivation and interbreeding with other close relations, yielding a range of domesticated, local varieties. There is a huge amount of plasticity in tea—seedlings from a single parent plant can produce variable offspring, and (very importantly) a single cultivar may grow differently in different environments. This flexibility allows the plants to adapt and survive under variable challenges from climates, pests, and soils. As a result, tea grows around the world in a wide range of conditions.

It may be that most of us will never have the opportunity or need to differentiate var. *sinensis* and var. *assamica*, since the majority of tea that can be grown in temperate regions of North America and the British Isles must be cold-tolerant. Pure var. *assamica* is unsuitable for growing unsheltered in these climates, given its susceptibility to cold winter weather. However, this does not preclude growing plants with var. *assamica* characteristics, since they readily hybridize with var. *sinensis* plants—many hybrids are growing all over the world! Our garden has several var. *assamica*–like tea plants growing under the shelter of trees. They were collected as seeds in various species gardens in southern China, so they cannot be considered pure cultivars. But they definitely have morphology and growth habits consistent with var. *assamica*. Some are more robust than others, but most are periodically damaged by severe cold then recover, growing back vigorously from the roots.

Other varieties and camellia species are also used to make teas. These include *Camellia taliensis*, also known as *C. irrawadiensis*, which can be found growing in Yunnan Province of southwestern China as well as in Myanmar and Thailand—it serves as a source for rare and expensive teas made from the so-called wild tea tree. Another, *C. ptilophylla*, also known as *C. pubescens*, has small hairs on new buds and the undersides of leaves and is native to southern Hunan and northern Guangdong Province, China. Sometimes called cocoa tea, *C. ptilophylla* has considerably lower levels of caffeine, deriving its name and stimulating activity from another alkaloid, theobromine, which is also found in chocolate. Cocoa tea is also called white hair tea, due to the striking contrast of pubescence on the maroon-colored new leaves.

As with var. *assamica*, some of these plants can be grown in temperate regions with care. Although probably not of great commercial value, they may be of interest to collectors and avid gardeners. Furthermore, they serve as a source of genetic diversity for breeding and research. At Camellia Forest, we are testing *Camellia ptilophylla* for cold hardiness in the Piedmont region of North Carolina. Over the years we've enjoyed small batches of delicious cocoa tea.

Most *Camellia sinensis* and close relations readily hybridize and are quite common throughout the landscape in southern and western China. This combination, which leads to widespread hybridization, means there are virtually no "pure" forms in cultivation. Even some "wild tea trees" are likely derived from earlier cultivation. Others may be closely related varieties (for example, *C. taliensis*) rarely cultivated but used locally for tea.

Recent studies of *Camellia sinensis* genetics prove that many of the unique features enjoyed in tea are a result of key developmental events over millions of years. Var. *sinensis* and var. *assamica* diverged between 0.38 and 1.54 million years ago. Growing evidence shows that var. *assamica* actually includes two groups—one found in southwestern China and another in India. A third variety, *C. sinensis* var. *cambodiensis*, appears to be a hybrid of var. *sinensis* and the Chinese var. *assamica*. Interestingly the Chinese var. *assamica* shows more genetic variability than the one found in India, including signs of crossbreeding with *C. taliensis*. Increased understanding of the relationships among the various domesticated-tea and wild-tea varieties will help tea growers and tea lovers alike, as these interactions could lead to improved resiliency in the face of environmental changes we'll face in years to come.

# TEA IN CULTIVATION

Over thousands of years, tea evolved through both environmental pressures and human cultivation. By contrast, the modern processes of selecting cultivated varieties for commercial production seems relatively short—but it can still take decades—and resulting cultivars are often highly treasured across the tea industry. *Camellia sinensis* var. *sinensis* grows widely throughout China, Japan, and Korea. Brought by the British to India in the nineteenth century, it's the original source of the popular Darjeeling tea grown in the foothills of

## ORNAMENTAL CAMELLIAS

Gardeners often ask whether the ornamental plants *Camellia japonica* and *C. sasanqua* can be used to produce tea. The short answer is no, because they lack the compounds that produce the tastes and aroma of processed teas. However, leaves from the hybrid *C. sinensis* var. *sinensis* × *C. japonica* are sometimes used for tea and yield a distinctively different taste and aroma. Over time, prior to the domestication of tea, closely related camellia species have shared genetic materials, however these events are rare, and intentional breeding shows low compatibility and few offspring.

While the health effects of tea from hybridized *Camellia japonica* and *C. sinensis* have been studied, I haven't found anyone selling it commercially or further guidance on the comparative qualities of the leaf. In our collection, we have a hybrid of *C. sasanqua* and *C. sinensis* called *C.* 'Katsuzumi'. The tea made from these leaves has a very potent flavor, which we have on occasion mixed with regular green tea. I find it delicious, but it is very different from regular tea.

New growth and a mature leaf from 'Super Sochi', a vigorous and cold-resistant cultivar of plants from the Caucasus Mountain region of Georgia.

the Himalayas. With the best potential for withstanding cold weather, var. *sinensis* plants were later imported for cultivation near the Caucasus Mountains along the Black Sea. A dedicated breeding program selected those specimens best adapted to survive lower temperatures. These plants form the basis of the twentieth-century tea industry in Turkey, which also flourishes along the Black Sea coast. Tea cultivars in Japan and Korea are also well adapted to colder temperatures. Japanese cultivars have made their way to Hawaii and California, while Korean tea has been planted in southern Atlantic US states, including "wild tea" seed collected from Jiri Mountain, Korea, which we grow at Camellia Forest.

In recent years, seed collected from tea plants from old fields of the Caucasus Mountain region have been imported in large quantities to the United States and planted in several locations in southern, southeastern, and Pacific Northwest states, as well as locations in Scotland. Our own 'Super Sochi' cultivar, from an earlier introduction at Camellia Forest, has shown robust growth and impressive hardiness to the extremes of climate experienced here in the North Carolina Piedmont region and plantings as far north as Maryland. The superior performance of this cultivar compared with our other seedlings of Sochi and Caucasus origins highlights how differently tea offspring can grow despite coming from a single lineage.

Specific tea cultivars have been selected through the ages by growers, and more recently by formal research programs established in important tea-growing countries like China, Japan, and India. It can take twenty to thirty years to breed and trial new cultivars, which are selected for the flavor and aromatic qualities they bring to processed tea, as well as yield and resistance to various environmental challenges, such as climate extremes or insect damage. In order to preserve their selected characteristics, cultivars are typically propagated as rooted cuttings to obtain plants with genetic materials identical to the parent plant. This is especially useful when seeking a uniform crop; plants that are synchronized also facilitate harvest.

On the other hand, plants grown from seed may have an early and sustained advantage as they produce a taproot (a single central root from which side roots grow) that extends deeper into the soil. Plants grown from seed show more genetic diversity, which provides a range of strengths and resistance to environmental stressors, but more variability in terms of yield, quality, and other characteristics. The proportion of tea grown from clones or seeds varies widely throughout the tea industry.

## WHAT A TEA PLANT NEEDS
## TO SURVIVE AND THRIVE

Tea evolved as an understory plant in regions with high rainfall, such as the Golden Triangle contiguous area of Laos, Myanmar, and northwest Thailand; around the world today, tea is cultivated in regions generally characterized by sufficient precipitation and a lack of extreme temperatures. Growth is best at temperatures between 68°F and 86°F. However, many varieties can tolerate lows between 5°F and 25°F during dormancy. Rainfall of 37–70 inches per year is ideal, preferably with an even distribution and adequate amounts in the growing season. However, irrigation can be used to supplement in drier climates or cope with potential drought. In all settings, good drainage and soil acidity remain the essential features for successful growth.

We don't include recommendations based on climate maps—there can be much variation in a small field, as microclimates provide highly localized harbors suitable for tea cultivation, and gardeners can create their own to a greater or lesser degree. An easy way to check if your tea growing will be successful is to look at which other plants do well locally. Is anybody growing ornamental camellias? If yes, then tea will grow under similar conditions. Do blueberries thrive in your area? If so, then your soil may also be suitable for tea.

Tea is successfully grown in a wide variety of soil types around the world, with the exception of hard clay or mostly sandy soils. About two-thirds of feeding roots are found in the top 12–16 inches of soil. Tea can be grown in areas unsuitable for cultivating other crops, including on steep hillsides and in rocky soils. As a natural understory plant, it will also grow in partial shade. Many plantations grow tea in the full sun, though some include occasional shade trees to moderate the heat.

Tea plants are typically ready for harvest within three to five years of planting, and can last up to fifty years in production or longer—some have survived hundreds of years, often under wild conditions. In regions near the equator, tea can be harvested year-round. Farther north (or south), tea plants enter a period of winter dormancy that depends on day length. Lower temperatures increase the length of dormancy. Therefore, depending on the latitude and temperatures, tea grown in cooler climates can yield a harvest of four to five flushes per year ("flush" is the term used to describe the new growth picked to make tea).

# The Chemistry in Your Cup

**ALL MAJOR TYPES OF TEA** come from *Camellia sinensis*—differences arise from chemical changes that occur as the fresh leaf is harvested, withered, and dried. Various processing steps influence the level of oxidation to create different types of tea, from green (unoxidized) to oolong (partially oxidized) to black (fully oxidized).

The periodic growth of the tea plant, or "flush" when it is harvested, yields a series of five to seven leaves per stem. New growth is hand-plucked depending on the type and quality of tea (though demand for higher production and efficiency has resulted in wider use of mechanical harvesting and processing methods). Generally, handmade artisan teas derive their higher quality in part through the precision of hand harvesting and human input.

Developing an understanding of the chemistry of the leaf during various steps isn't required to make delicious tea, but it can be helpful. Knowing more about the "why" behind the "how" provides insight into effectively balancing important factors. Tea processing can provide a lifetime of learning. Many books have been written about the chemical changes that tea leaves undergo before they get to your cup, so here we give just a brief introduction.

The initial pluck is a form of damage that begins a stress response in the leaf leading to many of the characteristics we enjoy when drinking tea. Compounds found in the fresh leaf are platforms for creating additional molecules. Manipulating the leaf through the various processes outlined in later chapters transforms these compounds into chemicals we associate with the colors, flavors, aromas, and subtle variations across the different kinds of tea.

Polyphenols are the most abundant and important bioactive compounds in the fresh tea leaf and may provide a natural defense against insects, birds, and animals, as well as conferring potential health benefits to tea drinkers. The amino acid L-theanine is a unique constituent, produced by the plant's roots and transported to new leaves. Produced only by the tea plant (and a few mushrooms), theanine is responsible for the relaxing feeling that comes from having a nice cuppa—it seems likely that the theanine in tea was of great help to Buddhist monks in their meditations. And as a bonus, tea is prized for its caffeine, which happens to be helpful for staying awake while meditating. Caffeine is an alkaloid produced in new leaves, and is more concentrated by weight in newer growth. Content varies in the dried leaves and prepared beverages; in dry weight, caffeine comprises about 2–5 percent of the leaf depending on the variety.

A tea shoot ready for plucking. The more mature third and fourth leaves are too tough for white and green tea but are sometimes used for black or oolong.

Individual cultivars and varieties have different chemical constituents. Climate and soils also contribute to variation in taste, and still, holding these constant, different tea plants can produce different-tasting tea. The greatest distinctions found between var. *sinensis* and var. *assamica* derive from the higher content of certain polyphenols and the ratio of tea polyphenols to theanine.

Tea plants also contain various carbohydrates and free sugars. Some, such as cellulose, give the plant structure and stability. Important pigments include chlorophylls (the pigment that provides green color and allows plants to photosynthesize) and carotenoids (plant pigments responsible for yellows, oranges, and reds). During growth, chlorophyll interacts with sunlight in the process of photosynthesis to provide the plant with energy; levels are variable across the different cultivars, and are also influenced by shading. They are important to the taste of green tea, and contribute to the color of the processed leaf.

Aromatic compounds make up a small fraction of the tea leaf, but play a key role in the final quality of tea. There are hundreds of chemicals intrinsic to the tea plant or formed during processing that contribute to the flavors and aromas of the tea we drink.

## THE BUZZ ON TEA

Purine alkaloids, also called methylxanthines, occur in many plants naturally known to have stimulating activity, including tea, coffee, and cocoa. They include caffeine, theobromine, and theophylline. These and other alkaloids are known for their bitter taste.

Many people want to know which type of tea has the most caffeine. The amount of caffeine in a brewed cup of tea depends on how tea leaves are harvested, processed, and prepared. Caffeine levels are highest in the youngest growth, so tea with a high proportion of young leaves and buds will have more caffeine per weight than a similar cup made from more mature growth. Oxidation during processing changes caffeine levels only slightly, increasing a small amount as other alkaloids are transformed into caffeine.

Bright new growth from the first flush of tea growing at Camellia Forest.

# IMPORTANT COMPOUNDS IN TEA

| COMPOUND | IMPORTANCE | AMOUNT AND DEVELOPMENT | (percents represent fraction of dry weight of extracted solids) |
|---|---|---|---|
| **AMINO ACIDS** (L-THEANINE) | L-theanine is unique to tea and the most important amino acid found in the tea plant. It imparts a relaxing feeling and contributes to umami taste and aroma. | 6% of dry weight. Develops in roots and is transported to new growth. Shading during growth increases levels. | |
| **METHYLXANTHINES** (CAFFEINE) | Caffeine contributes to bitterness and astringency. It imparts a stimulating effect. Other methylxanthines also occur in small quantities, including theobromine (as in chocolate). | 2%–5% of dry weight depending on variety. Levels are highest in the youngest leaves and early spring growth. Caffeine levels increase during withering. | |
| **CARBOHYDRATES** (SUGAR, PECTIN, CELLULOSE) | Soluble sugars contribute to the sweet taste of the tea infusion—compounds named glycosides, bound to sugar, are released soon after plucking. | 11% of dry weight. Cellulose and lignin increase with age of leaf. Enzymes responsible for glycoside release are highest in spring, corresponding to seasonal differences in aromas and flavors (for example, first flush). | |
| **CHLOROPHYLL** | Green pigment interacts with sunlight to support growth. It's important to the taste of green tea. | A small fraction of tea weight. Levels are impacted by variety and increase with shading. | |

| COMPOUND | IMPORTANCE | AMOUNT AND DEVELOPMENT | (percents represent fraction of dry weight of extracted solids) |
|---|---|---|---|
| **CAROTENOIDS** (HUNDREDS—INCLUDING ß-CAROTENE, LUTEIN, AND LYCOPENE) | Various pigments are transformed into aromatic molecules in processes influenced by solar withering and heat. | A small fraction of tea weight. Some intrinsic to leaf, others formed during processing. Higher levels in mature leaf plus degradation products formed during processing contribute to qualities of black tea. | |
| **POLYPHENOLS** | Flavanols, which include catechins, are the main phenolic compounds that contribute to astringency and bitterness of green tea. During oxidation, catechins are transformed to theaflavin and thearubigins, which contribute to the color and briskness of black tea. Catechins and theaflavins are the main antioxidant compounds in tea. | 30%–40% of dry weight. Polyphenols, and their transformation during processing, contribute important characteristics to the different types of tea. | |
| **LIPIDS** | Unsaturated fatty acids may contribute to fresh, green, or floral aromas associated with certain oolong teas. | 2%–4% of fresh leaf. Amounts and types vary in mature and new growth, and are influenced by nitrogen levels. | |
| **MINERALS/METALS** | Common elements in tea include potassium and calcium, along with various metals, oxalic, malic, and citric acid, and other nutrients important in the synthesis of polyphenols. | Mature tea leaves accumulate elements such as iron, manganese, fluorine, and aluminum, while new growth concentrates others, such as zinc, magnesium, and copper. Tea also accumulates heavy metals from soils, including lead and cadmium. | |
| **VITAMINS** | Vitamin C is commonly found in tea, especially green tea. Vitamin K is also found in substantial quantities. | Levels decrease during processing of black and oolong teas. | |

In addition to processing, the characteristics and quality of the produced tea depend on a wide range of other factors. Taste will vary by the type of plant, region, and soil micronutrients—even the weather in the weeks and days before harvest. The extent to which consumers can discern these differences depends on their background and training. To meet the expectation of consumers, known commercial blends depend on the fine senses of trained tea tasters to achieve the expected taste of any particular tea (for example, English, Irish, or Scottish breakfast teas). Experienced tea tasters and connoisseurs can identify the subtle differences in each batch of tea. Just as for wine, a strong culture exists that recognizes teas from specific regions with distinctly different taste and aroma profiles.

# A BASIC GUIDE TO GROWING AND PROCESSING TEA

# Planning and Planting

Starting your first tea garden is an exciting prospect, whether you're an experienced or novice gardener. You may be interested in trying just a few plants in the garden, or maybe you want to grow enough to supply a substantial portion of your own personal tea drinking, or maybe you're adding to a small farm or creating something new. The basic principles of planning, propagation, and planting apply to any garden, small or large, and tea is no exception. For tea, the most important considerations include having a suitable climate (or adapting to less suitable conditions) and acidic, well-drained soils. Tea takes years to mature, and it can be difficult to fix mistakes and frustrating to do over, especially when starting from scratch. In other words, it's worth taking the time to plan ahead.

Tea gardening requires slowing down and following nature's pace to meet the rhythm of the growing tea. In temperate climates, tea leaves emerge in spring following a long period of dormancy. Throughout the growing season, rain or shine, nature's cycles determine when you can pluck, weed, or plant. If you're excited to start making tea *now*, we recommend plenty of interim steps that can yield some nearer-term gratification, such as planting your own seeds or making a little tea from younger plants.

# Site and Soils

**WHETHER YOU ARE** installing a few plants in the garden, a hedge, or a field, there are a number of factors to consider in situating your tea plants. Most growers will be starting within the constraints of a given site, such as a backyard or existing field. While tea is highly adaptable within certain limits, some conditions and practices increase the likelihood of growing a healthy and vigorous plant.

Climate is one of the key determinants of whether you can grow tea outdoors. If you can find ornamental camellias growing in your neighborhood, you can certainly grow tea. Most tea plants will do best in USDA cold-hardiness zones 7 or higher. A few cultivars can, with care, tolerate lower winter temperatures. Many growers have tried to expand the limits of tea, though the feasibility of this depends on how many plants you're growing and what resources you have at hand. Proximity to oceans or other large bodies of water is often a moderating factor—many parts of the British Isles and coastal regions of the Pacific Northwest are zones 8 and above. Higher altitudes, while good for growing tea in more tropical environments, are a challenge in temperate climates. Microclimates, which, due to some mitigating factors, can be quite different from their surrounding environment, can also help tea plants flourish.

We often associate tea with tropical climates, which bring to mind heavy summer rains and high humidity. In all climates, humidity is an important determinant of how much rain a plant needs, because it impacts both transpiration—the process of water moving through the plant and evaporating from the leaves—as well as evaporation of water from the soil. Optimal humidity for growing tea is from 50 percent up to 80–90 percent. Humidity below 40 percent can inhibit growth.

## SITE

Every garden or farm has, by chance and design, its own microclimate. Where to plant your tea will depend on your particular site and general climate, with consideration of how to meet the needs of the plant throughout the year. Selecting a site isn't always simple, especially since we are usually constrained by the existing landscape.

In warmer areas, such as the southern United States, growers may want to plant to reduce the impact of mid- to late-day sun during the heat of summer. By contrast, in colder and more northerly areas, tea may benefit from planting on a south-facing slope, which enhances

This hillside tea garden at Camellia Forest is planted on a northeast-facing slope in a forest clearing.

growth in summer and warmth in winter. At lower altitudes in our southeastern climate, an optimal site includes partial shade year-round, for example from evergreen trees. Tea in the wild is an under-story plant, so it's adapted for growing on the edges of woodlands—but we recommend at least a half day of sun in the garden since deep shade will reduce the rate of growth. Tea plants grown in full sun produce the most leaf, but in colder climates this makes them more susceptible to winter damage and sunburned leaves. Flavors from sun- and shade-grown tea may vary somewhat, though the difference can be rather subtle depending on the processing.

Trees or structures also protect tea plants from winter cold and winds. In our garden, for example, we plant on a northeast-facing slope for shade during late afternoon summer sunshine, and trees provide early morning shade protection in winter.

Tea needs sufficient light during the growing season to promote growth. Optimal growth requires enough sun for photosynthesis to support leaf production. This is especially true if you plan to harvest.

At Camellia Forest, we recommend up to 50 percent shade for most camellias, including tea. Optimal levels are 30–40 percent at low elevations in a humid environment. There is an ongoing debate over the role of shade trees in the commercial tea industry, where their impact can influence the economic bottom line. Both too much shade and high-intensity sunlight can inhibit photosynthesis. Shade also impacts leaf temperature and humidity. These factors influence growth rate and leaf quality at harvest. In full sun, temperatures experienced by leaves can be substantially higher than optimal ambient levels for growth (68°F–86°F), so midday and afternoon shade may be useful.

In temperate climates, day length and the warmth from sunlight are key determinants of the active growing season. Winter dormancy occurs when daylight lasts less than eleven hours and low temperatures fall below 50°F for six weeks or longer. This has implications for commercial tea production, since day length determines how much tea can be harvested. For the rest of us, it's simply a reality to understand as we wait and enjoy our tea across the changing seasons.

In late afternoon, when sun is most intense, our tea plants are shaded by the surrounding pines.

## SOILS

Given an appropriate climate and sufficient light, the next most important determinant of successful tea gardening is having soil that's both well-drained and acidic. Tea grows in a variety of soils and settings around the world. For optimal growth, deeper soils are best (3 feet or more). Seedling taproots will grow many feet down into the earth, but many of the fine surface roots (and most of those on clonal plants) spread within the top foot of soil. Tea plantations are frequently sited on rolling hillsides—and growing on a slope can certainly increase drainage—but it isn't a requirement or a guarantee of success. Drainage on a slope can be compromised by a rising water table lower downhill.

Two sets of hillside rows come together where water is channeled in between to divert heavy rain flow.

In all settings, we recommend building up your topsoil and creating a slightly raised bed. Although tea will grow and even flourish in many soils, some types will require amendments for optimal growth. Sandy soils may need added compost or organic matter to help hold water. By contrast, heavy clay soils often have poor drainage. For growing tea in native soil with a lot of clay, we recommend adding a substantial amount of compost. In addition to improving drainage, this will provide an important source of nutrients, including nitrogen and other micronutrients. We don't recommend adding sand for drainage; you'd need a large volume of added sand to get the drainage of a sandy soil, and sand doesn't contribute nutrients. Pea gravel (or PermaTill, a lightweight commercial product made from expanded slate) is a better solution, because it will increase drainage and can also discourage voles from eating your plants' roots.

Poor drainage is one of the most common problems we see for home tea growers, especially those who have a new house or want to plant near a foundation. To avoid soggy soil, *plan ahead before you plant*! Get to know your soil and how your site responds to water. In addition to adding soil conditioners, you may need to make structural fixes to ensure sufficient drainage. A French drain can help smaller gardens when there's a good deal of runoff; this tidy solution diverts water flowing from downspouts or other impermeable surfaces. Larger plantings require a careful approach, planting along contours only if soil is well drained.

Half a pup (or about 6 to 8 inches) is a good height for raised beds.

## ADDING SULFUR TO LOWER YOUR PH

Elemental sulfur is very effective for bringing down a high pH, and it avoids the problem of adding unnecessary fertilizer. Online instructions for adding it to your soil are usually geared toward very large plantings, so here we translate them for the home gardener. For a single point decrease in pH (for example, 7 to 6), use about 6 ounces elemental sulfur or pellets per square yard of loamy soil. Use more for clay soils (about 9 ounces) and less for sandy soils (about 4 ounces). If you have more than a single point to decrease (for example, 7.5 to 5.5), we recommend multiple applications over time, rather than larger amounts. Elemental sulfur acidifies soil with the help of bacterial actions, so to be effective, soils should be warm, moist, and not compacted.

On our sloped field and hillside, drainage can be a problem after extensive rain. To encourage drainage, we constructed a raised bed, at least 6–8 inches high or greater. We also dug a small channel perpendicular to the rows and constructed a berm above the planting to divert excessive runoff. We've tried a couple variations and find that an open ditch works as well as a pipe, which can tend to clog. The ditch can be lined with stones or grasses to help keep erosion in check.

Tea grows best in slightly acidic soils (pH 4.5–5.5). Acidity impacts which nutrients are available. Tea plants may be able to grow in higher-pH soils, but they'll be less productive and more sensitive to nutrient deficiencies. If your soil tends toward basic, there are various amendments to consider. We use pelletized sulfur for major shifts of a point or more. Certain nitrogen fertilizers, such as those containing ammonium sulfate or diammonium phosphate, are acidifying. In the unlikely scenario that your soil is lower than pH 4.5, you may need liming.

Because soil pH is so important for tea, it's worth investing in testing up front and adjusting your soil pH as needed. Sometimes you can get the testing done through state laboratories—these may be costly, but they are also the most accurate and come with a full range of other interesting measures, such as macro- and micronutrients. There are also various kits for doing it yourself. If you discover your pH is too high after you already have the plant in the ground, we recommend amending gradually with multiple applications. For just a few plants in the garden or just slight decreases of pH (for example, 6 to 5.5), we recommend gradually adding an acidifying fertilizer, such as ammonium sulfate. These fertilizers are sold in garden centers under various brands as "food for acid-loving plants."

# When to Plant

**THE BEST TIME OF YEAR** to plant depends on your climate, site characteristics, and resources for protecting the young plant against climate extremes and drought. In areas where winters are relatively mild, like the North Carolina Piedmont region where we live, as well as other low-elevation regions throughout the southeastern and western United States, we recommend planting in autumn. Autumn planting gives roots time to get established with less stress from summer heat and drought. Although freezing temperatures and snow can damage new growth, the most important action is going on under the soil. With adequate mulching (several inches at least), roots will be protected.

In regions with cooler climates such as the British Isles, the Pacific Northwest coast, or higher elevations where summers are relatively mild, spring planting may work best because roots can begin growing and become established before winter. However, because roots take time to develop, tea that's planted in spring requires more careful attention to watering during the first summer. This is especially the case in drier climates. Growers who plant in spring should have a plan in place for watering multiple times per week (in winter, of course, when plants aren't growing, they require much less water). Some growers in the southern United States (for example, The Great Mississippi Tea Company) choose to plant out in spring and rely on irrigation systems to ensure the plants don't dry out in summer. We install irrigation with our new plantings at Camellia Forest, but after the first year generally only need it during the occasional summer drought.

## AT A GLANCE: GENERAL RULES FOR PLANTING

- Know your site, soil type, and drainage needs.

- Raised beds (at least 6 inches tall) with added compost will address many but not all drainage problems.

- On a slope, consider the need to direct runoff to minimize erosion and control the water table.

- If possible, send a soil sample to the state or other labs to ensure pH is not too high. For high pH (above 6) use amendments to lower to 4.5–5.5.

- Focus on improving the soil in a larger area than the actual plant hole—a 3- to 4-foot-square area per tea plant is sufficient.

- Spacing of multiple tea plants is ideally about 3 feet apart. As little as a foot of spacing will create a dense hedge in a shorter time, but may eventually reduce the growth and health of individual plants.

- Consider access to water, especially for a larger planting. Irrigation may be needed when you are starting out and during droughts.

# Selecting and Sourcing Plants

**WHEN YOU FIRST START** growing your own tea, you will need to decide whether to grow plants directly from seeds or to transplant young plants. Both can be purchased from any number of commercial sources, though you may have to hunt a bit (or consult our resources section at the back of this book).

Despite being the most commonly grown camellia in the world, tea plants are not always easy to find—at least not at your local garden center! This may simply reflect limited supply and demand—with demand having been limited by a lack of information on growing tea (most gardeners and tea drinkers have no idea that tea comes from a camellia). On the supply side, commercial tea growers have a reasonable interest in protecting their valuable cultivars, the result of decades of investment and growth, from competition.

Obtaining quality plant material requires knowledge, time, and resources. One day, "garden-variety" tea plants may become more widely available, but research will be necessary to identify which varieties provide the most successful experience for home growers. Generally, we recommend small-leaf tea plants (var. *sinensis*) for growers in temperate climates up to zone 7. Large-leaf varieties (var. *assamica*), which are more sensitive to cold, can be grown in warmer zones (and sometimes in colder zones with protection). Diverse tea varieties have become available to growers like ourselves and small farmers across North America and the British Isles, either through the sharing of personal collections or by purchasing seeds sourced from international growers through industry consultants. The size of the leaf is not as important as its sensitivity to extreme cold and response to light. At Camellia Forest, we are continually trialing our new acquisitions and favorite varieties, mostly var. *sinensis* plants, which are protected from cold because they stop growing sooner in fall and start later in spring. We also grow var. *assamica* plants to provide diversity in flavors for processed teas, as well as genetic materials for hybridizing and creating new plants that flourish in temperate regions.

One of the challenges in purchasing tea plants is determining whether the plants' source and type are clearly or correctly labeled. The misidentification of plants was frequently cited as a problem by our survey respondents. You can't always tell the qualities of a cultivar based on the appearance of leaves, and it's impossible to tell from the seeds. While growing plants directly from seed can be gratifying, it takes longer to grow and produce tea than starting with established plants. Given the three- to five-year timeframe before plants are mature enough for harvesting, purchasing one- to two-year-old plants provides a considerable head start; growing from seed may take 20–40 percent longer before you can start making your own tea.

There are several strengths and limitations to starting from seed versus cuttings. Because cuttings require access to plant material, they're not a practical option for most beginning growers. Understanding the process of propagation is important, even if only to know what to look for when sourcing plants. For growers interested in self-sufficiency, learning the different types of propagation methods will also increase options for future growth and resilience.

## HOW TO TRANSFER YOUR TEA PLANT FROM POT TO GARDEN

1. Start with a plant, at least one to two years of age. Larger plants can get you off to a faster start, assuming they have good branching structure.

2. Prepare the soil in at least a 3-square-foot area, adding organic matter (and sulfur as needed for pH adjustment).

3. Build a raised bed of 6–8 inches, and in the prepared bed, dig a hole large enough for the full pot with loosened soil on both sides and underneath.

4. Invert the pot, supporting the plant with one hand and gently squeezing and tapping all around the pot to help it out.

5. Holding it by the roots, carefully center the plant in the hole with the soil level to or above the level of the ground.

6. Gently loosen the rootball surface (if rootbound, consider more assertive measures).

7. Refill with dirt around the roots, taking care not to cover the base of the plant with new dirt.

8. Add a small amount of slow-release, balanced fertilizer (10-10-10), or wait until the next growing season.

9. Cover with mulch, for example pine bark or needles, with a margin of a few inches around the stem.

10. Water gently but thoroughly, repeating as needed depending on rainfall and temperature. Less watering is needed in autumn when the plants stop growing.

**ABOVE** When transplanting, dig a hole that is just deep enough for the pot.

**LEFT** Cover roots with a thick layer of mulch, being careful to leave a few inches bare around the stem.

# Starting from Seeds

**GROWING TEA FROM SEEDS** seems like it should be fairly easy, and it is—if you follow some basic steps to mimic what happens in nature. Tea seeds naturally fall from their capsules directly onto the soil and into the organic matter that accumulates under the plants. If kept moist, some will eventually germinate and set roots where they lie. We can always tell when we've missed collecting from a plant when seedlings start sprouting up in the paths the next year. They can be quite vigorous and crowded together, spreading out from under the mother bush. Besides harvesting the seeds, we maintain pathways free of seedlings, either by mowing them (by accident, usually) or, preferably, digging them up and finding them another space to grow.

So many seeds are hiding under the branches.

The time to germination (sprouting) depends on seed quality and other factors, such as soil temperature. On their own, tea seeds that "plant themselves" in autumn will stay dormant in the soil and germinate in spring. If seeds are planted by a grower and germinate in fall, the tender new growth needs to be protected from freezing temperatures (seeds can also be started indoors if they're kept moist and, once they sprout, under lights). Seedlings can be transplanted the following fall or spring. We don't recommend planting out seedlings in summer, but it may be possible if you are able to adequately protect them from harsh sunlight and keep them watered and weeded.

The most important determinant for success is to start with viable seeds! Tea plants produce seeds once a year, in autumn. The fruits begin to ripen when the plants stop growing, about the same time they come into flower. The timing depends on climate, latitude, and hemisphere. In North Carolina, we begin to see swelling green capsules side by side with flower buds in late summer. The fruits typically contain one to three large brown seeds about the size of a hazelnut, and it's easy to see how many seeds are in each capsule. Growth begins to slow down by late August, and by late September, some seed capsules begin turning brown and develop cracks through which the seeds will ultimately be released.

The main requirement for viable seed is to avoid prolonged exposure to dry air. We collect seeds by plucking the ripened capsules directly off the plant before they open and begin drying out. After removing the fruits from the plants, we bring them inside and let them sit on trays or baskets. As they dry, the husks split. We then shell them by hand and prepare them for cold storage and later planting. We can

**RIGHT** Seeds ripen about the same time flowers bloom in fall.

**BELOW** A ripe seed about to open near a flower bud.

do this because we're not a huge operation, and the process fits neatly into our regular routine harvesting. In larger operations, seeds may be collected after they fall out of their husks naturally onto the ground. Unfortunately, seed viability might be compromised if they are left too long and dry out.

Both small and large quantities of seeds can be purchased from commercial sources. Working with a reputable or known source is important for a couple reasons. First, seed from a producer who follows best practices for collection, storage, and shipping is likely to be of higher quality and viability. Second, you're more likely to get accurate information about the tea itself, the variety, and country or climate of origin. As tea becomes more of a commercial crop in North America and the British Isles, seeds may become more accessible. At the same time, as commercial interests begin to play a larger role in sourcing tea for growers, there will probably come a time when the best varieties will be patented and protected, either raising prices or limiting their availability. Exports of tea seeds or other plant materials are often restricted in countries where tea is an important economic resource.

Whether seeds are purchased or picked, they either need to be planted immediately or stored properly. Small quantities of seeds can be easily kept in a sealed plastic bag or container along with a moistened paper towel in the refrigerator (some refrigerators may not keep a constant temperature, so it's good to check regularly and make sure your seeds stay cool but don't freeze). This process, called stratification, mimics natural dormancy. Although tea seeds can clearly survive winter weather outside, it's better if they're not subjected to multiple freeze-thaw cycles in storage. We typically see good viability in our seeds for one year or more under these conditions. Occasionally we will even see seeds begin sprouting after a longer time in the refrigerator if they have been kept too moist. Stratification is not a requirement for germination, but tea seeds planted directly without going through cold storage will tend to grow more slowly. From a survival perspective, stratification makes perfect sense. Seedlings sprouting in fall to winter may be more vulnerable to cold damage, and so they are more likely to make it if they take their time and wait for spring.

Tea seeds come with all the nutrients needed for producing a seedling. They are also sometimes used to produce oil. In China, tea seed oil is thought to be an especially nutritious supplement. I often imagine that these large seeds make a particularly good meal for an animal, since they are also full of carbohydrates and other nutrients. Indeed, when we planted out large amounts of seed in trays one year, some mysterious holes appeared and the seeds disappeared. We covered the beds with mesh and set out traps, but saw no further evidence of the bandit. While I've never seen squirrels collecting tea seeds from the plants, we have found tea plants growing on their own in the woods near our garden, perhaps cached and misplaced by a forgetful forager.

**OPPOSITE** Ripe seed capsules come in many shapes and sizes.

# HOW DO I KNOW IF MY SEEDS ARE GOOD?

You can test seeds for viability before planting, either directly after harvest or after a period of stratification. In the sink-float test, seeds are placed in a container of water. Those that sink after soaking for twenty-four hours are the most viable. Intermediate sinkers and floaters can be left in the water for another twenty-four to forty-eight hours, then all but the floaters can be planted. To rescue floaters, you can try putting them under a layer of moist sand then repeat the sink-float test after a day or two. Floaters may still germinate, but at a lower rate. They can still be planted if you have the space for them or need to make the best of a marginal batch of seeds. However, overall uniformity of seedlings is improved by stratification and selecting seeds that pass the sink-float test.

A mass of seedlings in a deep tray.

Seedling taproots need more depth to grow straight, but will reorient on repotting or planting out.

# Methods for Preparing Seeds

**THERE ARE SEVERAL METHODS** to prepare tea seeds for planting. When you have only a few seeds and are unsure about viability, one option is to place seeds in a sealed plastic bag with a moistened paper towel until they crack and begin to send out a root. This keeps the seeds reliably moistened and provides an opportunity to peek in the bag to see how well the seeds are sprouting. While this can be educational, we haven't seen any evidence that it actually speeds up germination compared with planting directly in soil. This method also increases the possibility that the seeds will mold.

Choosing the best setup for growing seeds depends on how many you're trying to grow, your infrastructure and supplies, and the time you have to actively maintain and nurture the growing seedlings. Planting in trays or beds is good for larger amounts of seed. This minimizes the space and time required for preparation, watering, and maintenance. Individual pots or cell packs, on the other hand, are good for smaller numbers of seeds and are somewhat more efficient when repotting or transplanting to the garden. Planting seeds directly in the garden allows the taproot to grow undisturbed, but these seeds require more care in the short term to keep them sufficiently moist and free of weeds. Seeds planted outdoors also need to be protected from disturbance by animals, including field mice, voles, squirrels, and larger mammals, such as humans, who might inadvertently step on your beds.

Fresh, weed-free soil is especially necessary for germinating seeds. This can be purchased as a mix specifically formulated for camellias or azaleas. For growers who enjoy making their own mix, the goal is to create an acidic soil of about pH 5 that will provide good drainage. It should hold some moisture, but not too much. We use a mix of two-thirds aged pine bark and one-third peat moss. In the southeastern United States, pine bark is a common soil conditioner. In other parts of the country, other components may be more accessible, such as aged fir bark in the Pacific Northwest. Consult your local garden center or agricultural extension agent to learn about which media are best for your region. Adding good compost to the mix can be helpful, but it should be finely sieved since the small particles help hold water. Many commercial potting mixes are rich in peat moss, which holds water and so may cause the soil to stay too wet. Adding perlite (expanded pumice) or sand may help. Caution is needed to avoid overwatering in peat moss–based soils.

Seeds come with their own store of nutrients, but fertilizer can be added to the soil to improve growth over a longer period of time. We usually supplement our soils only after the seedlings are transplanted, since successful germination doesn't require external nutrients to stimulate early root growth. If seedlings are left in place for longer than a few months, growth will eventually slow as available nutrients are used up. We recommend a slow-release, balanced (10-10-10) fertilizer, or starting out with a good compost in the soil mix.

## GROWING TEA FROM SEEDS IN POTS

Seeds don't need to be planted very deep, no more than ½ inch into the soil, before covering. If you're starting your seeds in a pot or a tray, start by adding soil up to ¾ inch from the top of the container. Place a seed on top and cover with ½ inch of soil. For a large tray, you can evenly disperse a large number of seeds and add a loose layer of soil to evenly cover them, gently compressing the soil so the seeds aren't disturbed by watering. For a smaller number of seeds, you can make individual holes in the soil and then cover.

After planting, the seeds continue to need protection from drying out. This is probably the biggest source of failure we see when people try to germinate tea seeds. You can water them regularly by hand or use a small overhead sprinkler as needed. Moisture in the soil should be monitored so that no more than the surface dries out. But don't overwater or the seeds will rot. You can also purchase plastic domes to fit over the trays, or use sealed plastic bags over the pots to maintain humidity. Keep seeds out of direct sunlight, under shade if outdoors, or inside. Choose a place you can regularly monitor them for moisture. Seeds will start more slowly in winter or colder weather, but may speed up a bit if they are kept warm (around 70 °F). A seedling heat mat may help—and as a bonus, heat mats are useful later when processing black tea.

When seeds sprout, they first send a root out into the soil; then a shoot with leaves will appear. You must to continue to keep them moist. The seedlings will need greater light exposure when the leaves emerge, but should be kept out of strong sunlight to prevent drying out. You can keep your seedlings in pots or trays for several months (up to a year), or transfer them to larger pots. Repotting with fresh

These seeds are about ½ inch below the surface and ready to be covered with soil.

A lot is happening underground as the seedling begins to sprout—be patient and keep the soil moist.

## WHAT ABOUT THE TAPROOT?

Germinating seeds will send down a taproot, which ultimately grows as deep as several feet and provides an early advantage and hardiness under variable climate stressors such as drought. But in a tray or pot, taproots can easily become overgrown. When the taproot hits the bottom of the container, the tip of the growing root may die, coil around the inside, or become tangled, coming out the drainage holes. Even if the taproot stays healthy in a pot, it can be difficult to preserve when transplanting. The good news is that wherever it is broken, many smaller roots develop above the break. Sometimes growers even remove the taproot specifically to encourage development of a more fibrous root system, which is actually better if your long-term plans are to grow the tea in pots.

Seedling with a taproot.

These seedlings only need a little boost of fertilizer to start growing.

The seedling on the left started out about the size of its neighbors; ten months after being transplanted, it has grown significantly.

When transplanting seedlings, carefully center the stem so the depth is the same as it was before transplanting.

**Pots or packs** Some growers prefer the cell pack because it allows for easier transplanting of individual seedlings (assuming the roots haven't grown out the drain hole). We prefer pots, in part because they can be reused; cell packs can be deformed or broken when extracting seedlings. Biodegradable pots, while a good idea for shorter-germinating plants, aren't suitable for tea because they don't stay moist enough to last from germination to planting.

**Trays** Larger quantities of seeds may be easily grown in a tray and placed close together (for example, an inch apart), which allows roots to grow freely in any direction. Trays are made in a variety of sizes and depths. The ideal depth depends on how quickly you plan to transplant, but we recommend 3–4 inches if seedlings will be planted within six months or less. Seedlings grown in shallow trays need to be moved sooner to provide space for the roots.

Because seeds regularly volunteer when they drop under the plants, we once thought it would be fairly easy to grow a row of seedlings directly in the garden. We started in late spring. On a nice raised bed, we laid out a weed barrier with irrigation tape along the row, planting seeds through premade holes in the cloth. One especially hot and dry week in early summer, we forgot to add the seedling row to the watering schedule. In the weeks to come, the only seeds that germinated were those in the shady corner at the end of the row.

When we finally got around to replanting in fall and removed the weed barrier cloth, we found another surprise—vole trails leading to most of the remaining seed holes, and no seeds! That summer, the voles had invaded other parts of the garden, too, finding shelter along the irrigation lines. After adding PermaTill to the soil, we replanted the row. We didn't irrigate over winter, and by the next spring we had nearly 100 percent germination and a long line of seedlings, many of which continue to flourish today.

soil or adding fertilizer will stimulate a seedling to continue growing. When transplanting, gently remove the seedling from its container and shake off excess soil. Keep the roots from drying out as you prepare to transplant it into the new soil. When you place the seedling, situate it so the stem will emerge from the new soil at about the same depth as when it was in the seed tray or cell. Fill the pot partially with soil before centering the seedling and gently filling around the root to about 1 inch from the rim of the pot, tamping gently to firm the soil, then watering.

## GROWING TEA FROM SEEDS IN THE GARDEN

Seeds can also be planted outdoors in a special bed (rather than a tray) or directly in the garden wherever you want them to grow. In either case, the soil must be carefully prepared to minimize the growth of weeds, and marked well to prevent it from being disturbed during germination and early growth. Weed-free compost, aged pine bark, sand, or other soil amendments can be added, following the same principals of acidity (i.e., pH 4.5–5.5) and drainage as for growing in pots. Raised beds can help with drainage.

To maintain soil moisture during and after germination, you can protect seed beds with a hoop or temporary structure or cover them to provide shade and reduce drying out. During early growth stages, this cover may be sealed, but you must be able to access the soil easily to check moisture and seed germination. Once the seedlings emerge, the structure can remain in place with plastic removed and shade gradually reduced. It's best to gently water the seedling beds by hand or with a light sprinkler.

You can customize the size and design of the seedling bed and shade structure in countless ways. We prefer a sturdy and reusable hoop structure made of bent PVC pipe or electrical conduit and covered with a layer of shade cloth and plastic as desired. Other options include bamboo or another natural material that can be bent to provide a sturdy structure. Simpler designs could utilize salvaged windows or doors resting on a structure surrounding a raised bed. However, you must avoid overheating your enclosed structures so you don't cook the seeds!

Some growers plant directly in the garden to avoid the need for transplanting and maximize the likelihood that the taproot will survive. As with trays or pots, the seeds are planted ½ inch into the

## AT A GLANCE: GROWING TEA FROM SEED

### PREPARING SEEDS

- Obtain seed, test for quality

- Sink-float test; discard floaters or plant separately

- Store, keeping moist and cool, or plant directly as desired

- Stratify (cold treatment) to increase uniformity and germination rate

### PLANTING

- Prepare infrastructure and soil

- If using containers, fill with well-drained soil (for example, aged bark plus compost)

- If planting directly in the garden, prepare well-drained acidic soil and protect from erosion

- Place seeds atop soil, cover with thin layer (½ inch)

- Time for seed germination depends on season and stratification

### PROTECTION AND MAINTENANCE

- Place pots or trays in the shade or shade them using fabric, bamboo leaves, grasses, or a protected site

- Protect from animals and human disturbance

- Water, watch, and wait for 6 to 8 weeks

- Keep moist with sprinklers, misting, or other regular gentle watering

- Weed before and after as needed

- Option: cover with plastic to reduce evaporation

soil. Multiple seeds can be planted in one location, increasing the chance of having at least one plant at that site and sometimes producing composite bushes with multiple stems.

You may want to install drip irrigation at the same time you plant your seeds. Not only does this help keep young plants alive but the setup can also be useful in future years for watering during dry periods. The bed can be protected by a raised screen or netting to keep out critters. Protection from voles is also important, either with barriers around the field or measures to protect individual plants.

# Growing Tea Plants from Cuttings

No taproot on this clone, but plenty of root growth to expand and support the plant.

**VEGETATIVE, OR CLONAL,** propagation is a widely used method for growing tea. There are a few good reasons people choose this method. Starting with cuttings provides a head start; a plant grown from a cutting taken in July will be further along for planting the following year compared with a seedling started at the same time. And since plants grown from seed often have different characteristics than their parent, choosing clonal propagation ensures that once you've identified a plant you want to replicate, you know exactly what you're getting with future plantings.

Long-term plant-breeding and selection programs have developed clones for commercial production in many countries, but these are highly protected and difficult to export. No systematic breeding programs exist in North America or the British Isles, though as tea becomes more profitable, more organizations may become interested in funding this research. Suitability for various regions will need to be evaluated over a long enough time frame to allow for typical climate variations. For this reason alone, using plant materials that have been proven to flourish locally is the best option for most growers.

One of our goals at Camellia Forest has been to obtain a diverse selection of tea plants from around the world, testing them in our local climate and selecting the most vigorous and hardy plants. Some of our collection has been growing on site or nearby for several decades (or more, in the case of a small-leaf tea plant we obtained from a local collection, which was probably brought from Japan a century ago). Other regional growers may have access to plants grown by earlier generations, which are survivors in that particular climate. We encourage both formal and informal trials in various environments. Long-term trials are needed to identify the best plants for different climates, for example the hot and humid southern United States, western states where summers are typically drier and often hot, or the colder, more northerly maritime climates such as the British Isles. A collaborative spirit is the key to a supportive community of growers and breeders; only through openness and sharing can we promote development of regionally adapted cultivars.

The general principles of clonal propagation are simple but fascinating. Root development is an automatic response stimulated when a stem is wounded. The outer cells of the stem die and underlying cells form a visible swelling called a callus. Roots then begin to form from the vascular tissue of the stem or from the callus. Plant hormones, which help stimulate this growth, are naturally transported from the growing part of the stem (you can also apply a synthetic version when you make the cutting). Rooting time ranges from one to three months. Unlike seedlings, clonal plants have a diffuse root system rather than a central taproot.

We find that the most successful tea cuttings are taken from semihardwood (shoots that have aged enough so the stems have changed from green to brown) on the current year's growth, typically in early summer. Look for shoots that end in a terminal bud—this indicates that they are beginning to harden (find more information on terminal buds and growth patterns in our discussion of harvesting). Cuttings can be made later in the year, but may not root as quickly or efficiently. Some growers have success with softwood (green) cuttings, but use caution here—the young stem may root faster but is more prone to rotting. I also know someone (an expert in bonsai) who was able to root with moderate success from branches pruned off dormant plants in winter.

Take your cuttings from semi-hardwood and just above a leaf.

Multi-leaf shoots with a terminal bud and a good stretch of bare stem (1-inch minimum) for sticking in the soil make ideal cuttings.

Single-leaf cuttings are one solution to limited plant material, but they yield a smaller plant and start growing more slowly.

We like to use a multi-leaf cutting, which provides more energy to the growing root through an increased capacity for photosynthesis and can also lead to improved branching and formation of the mature plant. Multi-leaf cuttings require careful attention to watering due to their greater leaf surface area and need for added moisture while roots are forming. Some growers use single-leaf cuttings as a way to get more plants from the same amount of material. This high-throughput method is used in larger commercial plantations with great success. There's no guaranteed best approach for beginners, but with proper attention to watering, the multi-leaf cutting will tend to move the process along faster.

A well-planned setup is critical to successful clonal propagation; you should have a system in place to keep the cuttings moist while they are forming roots. Prepare containers by soaking them overnight in a dilute bleach solution (one part bleach to nine parts water) to reduce contamination by soil fungi and bacteria. If you use frequent misting or watering, you'll need soil with good drainage—we use a mix of aged pine bark and perlite (for example, two parts bark to one part perlite or sand by volume). Peat moss mixed with perlite is useful for setups with irregular watering. Avoid added compost or manure, which may grow fungi. Fertilizer can include a small amount of slow-release N-P-K (though the nitrogen isn't needed at first) or super-phosphate. Soil should have a low pH (4.5–5.5), as a higher pH encourages greater development of the callus and may reduce root growth. You can lower soil pH by adding sulfur, aluminum, or ferrous sulfate. If you're still having trouble, also consider the pH of your water.

It's important to prevent the leaves from drying out when you take cuttings. Start in early morning when dew is on the plants and before the sun hits the leaves, or choose a cloudy and cool or rainy day. Place cuttings in a plastic bag, spraying water inside the bag to maintain moisture levels. Ideally, cuttings should be planted within a day or two, but they can last several days or weeks if kept both moist and cool.

Make cuttings using a sharp knife or pruning shears sterilized in alcohol. Make the initial cut at an angle, leaving enough stem to be able to stick about an inch into the soil. If the leaves are close together, you may need to remove some lower leaves to have enough stem to stick in the soil. Growth hormones, such as IAA (indole acetic acid) or IBA (indole butyric acid), can help with successful cloning. We like ones that can be purchased as a powder (for example, Hormodin 2) and used without diluting—simply dip the cut end in water and then

the dry powder before sticking the stem in soil. We've seen recommendations for other practices, such as dipping the stem in honey, which may have antifungal or antibacterial properties, reducing the possibility the stem will rot.

Once you stick the cutting in the soil, it needs to be kept moist until the roots grow. In our greenhouses, we run our mist system every eight minutes for ten seconds. On a smaller scale, you can buy various trays with sealed plastic lids or rig your own out of a large jar placed over the soil or plastic bag tented and sealed around the pot. As with seeds, warmth is good for growth, but keep the pots or trays out of the sun so they don't dry out. If you are planting in a tent system with less access to regular water, you may also want to experiment with single-leaf cuttings or cut off parts of the leaves to reduce transpiration.

## AT A GLANCE: PROPAGATING FROM CUTTINGS

### PREPARE INFRASTRUCTURE AND SOIL

- Identify and sterilize pots or trays and associated watering system

- Use well-drained, acidic soil: a bark and perlite mix for regular watering, peat moss and perlite mix for under a dome

- Fertilize with low rates of superphosphate or slow-release fertilizer (optional)

- Identify plant material, preferably from a young plant with active shoots

- Best in June or July, but any-time is okay—semihardwood or softwood

- Work in the early mornings or on cool, cloudy, or rainy days

- Plan ahead to keep leaves moist, using a handheld mister as needed

### TAKE CUTTINGS

- Use sharp pruning shears or a knife—spray blades with 70 percent alcohol to sterilize

- Cut multi-leaf or shoots (for making single-leaf cuts at later point)

- Keep cuttings in a moist plastic bag and use a cooler for transport or storage if it will be more than a couple hours before sticking

### STICK CUTTINGS

- Dip end of cutting in rooting solution

- Stick ¼ to ¾ inch into soil

### PROTECT AND MAINTAIN

- Shade using fabric or situate in a protected site

- Tent cuttings if you'll be watering less frequently

- Maintain moisture for one to three months while rooting

# SEEDS VERSUS CUTTINGS

| | SEEDS | CUTTINGS |
|---|---|---|
| **ADVANTAGES** | Promotes diversity, resilience, and opportunities for new selections<br><br>Relatively inexpensive to start<br><br>Taproot can increase resiliency<br><br>No special infrastructure needed<br><br>May be planted directly in garden | Promotes uniformity<br><br>Clones and cultivars with established quality<br><br>Large numbers can be produced rapidly<br><br>Multi-leaf cuttings can provide a headstart |
| **DISADVANTAGES** | Inconsistent seed viability depending on harvest procedures and post-harvest handling<br><br>Inconsistent seedling quality<br><br>Taproot may not survive transplanting | Limited availability of source material for new growers<br><br>Uniformity may reduce a garden's resiliency<br><br>Mist or other system may be necessary to maintain moisture |
| **KEY DETERMINANTS OF SUCCESS** | Seed viability and quality<br><br>Consistent moisture<br><br>Well-drained soil | Taken from growing shoots<br><br>Proper setup for keeping leaves moist during propagation |
| **TIMING** | Takes six to eight weeks to germinate | Takes between two and three months to root |
| **SIMILAR SETUP AND CARE** | Containers or in-ground beds<br>Acidic, weed-free soil; limited fertilizer<br>Protection from animal and human disturbance<br>Constant source of moisture (mist, sprinkler, tent)<br>Careful control of weeds during and after sprouting/rooting | |

# Caring for Your Tea Plants

The three most important requirements for successfully growing your own tea are planning, patience, and persistence. Planning your tea garden involves balancing your goals and resources and working within the limits of any given site. There are many ways to optimize your success by planning. First, get to know your site and soil. Adjust your pH if necessary and plan for drainage. Plan for watering by hand or irrigating in the first few years. Plan for cold. Plan for heat. Plan for pests, critters, and weeds. Then cultivate your patience as you wait for these slow-growing plants to mature. It helps to have a persistent and positive outlook to go along with your patience as you put in the upfront effort before enjoying your tea in the years to come.

The rewards for all this are amazing. But it can be hard to wait! While you plan for planting, you can enjoy growing tea as a potted plant. Potted plants are easy to move indoors to prevent freezing in winter, and maintaining tea in a pot will give you a chance to get to know the plant. Though tea does best when planted in the ground, starting your tea in pots is certainly better than planting it out and then having to move it or remedy the site with the plant in place. In this chapter, we'll discuss all the stages of caring for your tea plants, from the earliest years to the most mature.

# Establishing Healthy Plants (Years One and Two)

**THERE ARE SEVERAL** important tasks that are crucial to your plant's success in the early years. These include formative pruning, fertilizing, watering, and weeding. We'll break down the details of each task and then summarize the steps in a handy quick-reference timeline.

## PRUNING

Formative pruning is an essential part of caring for young tea plants. Traditional formation involves a series of steps over several years that will eventually yield a plant with a strong "frame" (sturdy foundational branches), supporting as many shoots as possible growing out of the "plucking table" (the level from which pluckable shoots emerge—in some traditional tea plantations this may actually resemble a flat table). The good news is that pruning during the growing season yields a short-term reward: you can keep the trimmings and make them into tea—no waiting!

If you purchased your plant, you will be dependent on whatever formative pruning was done in the nursery. If you're starting from seed or your own clonal propagation, you'll want to begin formative pruning early. At Camellia Forest, we prune at least twice during the initial twelve to eighteen months of growth. First, we cut the central growing stem at about 6–10 inches from the ground to promote branching. For us this is often during summer when the plant is actively growing, but not too late in the season, which could stimulate late growth and sensitivity to frost in winter. If the plant only has one stem, which is often the case, cutting on the higher side will promote branching and preserve the plant's functional leaves. One name for this first cut is decentering. Its purpose is to break apical dominance, a physiological state in which hormones in the dominant growing stem actively suppress the growth of lateral branches. After breaking apical dominance, lateral buds begin to grow into stems. These new shoots will eventually develop their own apical dominance, suppressing further branching. This process plays an important role in the cycle of new growth and subsequent shoots you can pluck. If the plant has other mature (tall) branches, we trim them back to about the same height as the central stem. This promotes even more branching.

This plant, at about ten months, has had its first cut (decentering) to promote branching.

We often decenter our plants in pots (growing them in the pot for two years works best in our climate), but you can also decenter after planting in the ground. Some growers do the first decentering directly after planting out to alleviate transplant shock, reducing (in theory) the demands and stresses on the plant. This might be helpful in places with very hot summer temperatures and full sun. When the plant is in the ground, you can also do formative pruning during the winter dormant period. Seedlings can grow at different rates—to get them all the same height, those with tough stems may need to be cut with sharp pruners while those with more tender shoots may be plucked by hand.

For vigorous seedlings planted in spring, you can break off the tender new growth of the central stem once it reaches about 12–18 inches (probably midsummer). Weak plants should be left intact throughout the full growing season and decentered the following winter. Clonal plants (vs. seedlings) may benefit from growing longer in the garden before decentering.

In year two (or three, if you started later), you should perform a second formative pruning, cutting about 2–3 inches above the initial decentering (the stub from the prior cut will remain just above where branching occurred). The idea is to continue to stimulate branching and create a wider, lower frame than if the plant was allowed to grow in its natural form as a large and often leggy shrub. Not only does this provide more opportunities for pluckable shoots in later years, it also creates a strong frame to support the branches under snow or ice so they don't split or break from the main stem under too much weight. This step can be repeated in year four (or five).

Finally, while it isn't critical in early stages, some growers also remove the lowest leaves or small branches on the bottom 1–3 inches of the main stem. You can do this when you decenter or later if you have very few branches. The idea is to reduce the lateral branches at ground level, which aren't useful for plucking and can reduce airflow and plant health. I also prune these types of branches on my older plants to increase air flow and give pesky voles less cover.

## FIRST FORMATIVE PRUNE

Here we see the initial formation cut (decentering) that will stimulate the young tea plant to branch and the expected growth during the same season.

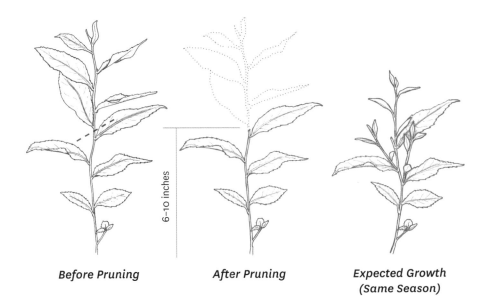

*Before Pruning*  *After Pruning*  *Expected Growth (Same Season)*

## SECOND FORMATIVE PRUNE

As the plants grows, subsequent cuts will continue to encourage branching

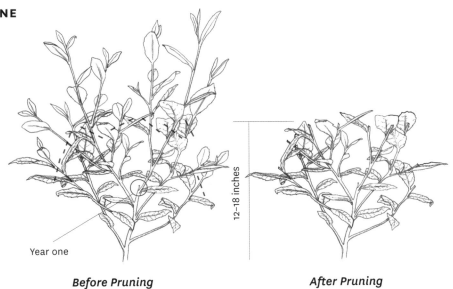

Year one

*Before Pruning*  *After Pruning*

Just a little trim off the top means more to harvest in the months to come. Note the new growth starting just below the cut.

## AT A GLANCE: PRUNING TIPS

*Pruning can be intimidating, but following these simple steps will help give you a more productive tea plant in the years to come.*

- Use clean, sharp tools— hand pruners for smaller stems or loppers for larger ones. If you have a lot of plants, sharp power shears may be okay for light trimming.

- For larger stems, cut at an angle just above a lateral branch.

- For smaller stems or for trimming, cut below the terminal branches close to the next lowest lateral branch or leaf.

- Directions are guidelines. Use your best judgment based on the health of the plant, its initial growth, and desired shape and height.

### DECENTER TO FORM THE FRAME AND PLUCKING TABLE (TWELVE TO EIGHTEEN MONTHS)

- Identify previous pruning sites and the most recent cut and look for a central dominant stem or stems (usually at least ¼-inch diameter).

- Cut the central growing stem at about 6–10 inches from the ground (or higher if you want a taller frame).

- If tea was planted in summer or fall, do this in late winter.

- If tea was planted in spring, do this as early as midsummer, or the following winter.

- Avoid cutting in later summer and fall, as it may stimulate growth that could be vulnerable to early frosts.

- Use sharp pruners if the stem is woody, or snap with your fingers if the stem is still green.

- If needed, trim lateral branches to the same height as the main stem.

### FRAME-FORMATION PRUNE (YEAR TWO OR THREE; REPEAT AT YEAR FOUR OR FIVE)

- Cut central branches back to about 2–3 inches above the first pruning.

- Side branches (nondominant) can be left at their original length or trimmed as desired. When plants are larger, the longer side branches can be cut back as needed and lower branches removed, especially those that reach the ground.

# FERTILIZER

Fertilizer is helpful in promoting healthy roots and vigorous growth. Nitrogen (N) makes an essential contribution to the growing leaf, while phosphorous (P) plays a role in supporting the root growth, and potassium (K) is important for the vigorous growth of young plants, as well as helping them withstand drought and cold. When growing tea in pots, we use a slow-release, balanced fertilizer, such as 10-10-10 (N-P-K), or one with a relative abundance of nitrogen (for example, 12-4-8), especially as the plants grow and are harvested regularly. Once the plants go in the ground, we use less fertilizer but more often, typically in early spring, late spring, and midsummer.

Fertilizer should be spread in the radius of the plant where the feeder roots are growing. This may be as small as a few inches on each side of a transplant or as wide as 12–18 inches around the trunk of a more mature plant. While a balanced fertilizer may be convenient, there are times that individual nutrients may be necessary, particularly if soil testing identifies a deficiency.

Sometimes plants need a boost of nitrogen. Bloodmeal is rich in nitrogen, water-soluble, and relatively fast-acting. The scent is supposed to repel some animals (herbivores, mostly) but may attract others. My dog, for example, becomes very interested in the tea garden whenever we use it. Along a similar line is fish meal—it's somewhat lower in nitrogen, but smellier. Take care in applying, as too much nitrogen may "burn" the plants.

Due to its importance in supporting root growth, we recommend incorporating phosphorous into your soil before planting. While it can be added later, it should never be dug into soil around a tea plant as this will damage the feeder roots near the surface. Instead, you can poke holes in the soil with the tines of a fork and spread the fertilizer on the surface of the soil nearby. Availability is increased at a slightly higher pH (5.5–7) and in the presence of mycorrhizal fungi (a special type of fungi that colonize plant roots and help with nutrient uptake). Unless you have a deficiency identified by soil testing, additional phosphorous is rarely needed. In excess, it may be damaging to plants and the environment.

Organic fertilizers help improve soil at many levels. We recommend worm compost or aged manure. Organic fertilizers, though lower concentration than most synthetic options, will provide sufficient N, P, and K, and will help with micronutrients as well. Having high organic matter in the soil to start, and using organic mulches, is critical to maintaining the nutrients needed for growing tea. Pruning sometimes generates a substantial amount of plant waste that could make effective organic mulch, but leaving branches where they fall is not terribly attractive in the garden. Furthermore, we found that a layer of organic debris under the plants compounded a problem we were having with voles, which love the cover. A better idea, which balances the need for formative pruning, is to compost trimmings elsewhere and return the compost to the garden in a finer form.

## WEED CONTROL

Weed control is important, especially for larger plantings like a hedgerow. Weeds are typically more vigorous compared with the slow-growing tea plant. In theory, some types of weeds or grasses may provide needed shade for young tea plants. But they can also compete for nutrients, and many are unwelcome visitors in residential gardens. The feeder roots of the tea plant are shallow, so *gentle hand-weeding* is critical. Do not till, hoe, or otherwise cultivate the soil near tea plants, as it will disturb these surface roots.

Prevention is key. Remove as many of the weeds as possible before you plant, and do your best to keep them from reseeding.

Pine needles make a very effective mulch, and fresh needles are a lovely contrast against the background of a new planting.

Besides hand-weeding, there are a variety of weed-suppressing techniques. The two most common methods are ground cloth and mulch. Both help maintain moisture in the soil. Ground cloth is a good short-term solution when starting with very young plants. However, weeds will have their way, and many eventually figure out how to grow on top of or through the cloth.

Several years ago, we planted a row of seeds on a bed covered with ground cloth (with holes punched in it over the seeds). A storm dislodged the cloth and we had to reinstall it with extra anchoring. Eventually it began to support weeds, so we put mixed wood bark on top to suppress them. Within another year, the best I can say is that although the weeds are still sprouting, they're easier to pull, as most of the roots are limited to the decomposing mulch rather than deeply anchored in the soil.

In most cases, mulch is preferable to ground cloth, as it contributes to long-term soil health. Pine needles or bark are ideal. After years of experimenting with different options, we found pine needles to be a very effective choice. As they slowly break down, they help with soil acidity. Your local options may vary. For example, in the Pacific Northwest, Douglas fir bark may be more accessible. Some landscapers recommend sawdust or woodchips, but decomposing hardwood can cause a rise in soil pH. We've seen this with mixed-wood mulch as well, so both are best avoided. Take care to not let the mulch get too close to the stem of the plant—surface roots need air, and mulch decomposing too close to the bark can invite rot.

Some tea growers may want to use a green mulch, also called a cover crop or interrow crop. When tea reaches maturity, it will begin to shade out the weeds around its base. Tea plantations use narrow aisles to shade out weeds while maximizing production. By contrast, some gardeners or small-scale farmers find that wider aisles and green mulches such as grasses or clovers can be an attractive and practical way to suppress weeds. These can be mowed, and, if left to compost in place, add organic material back to the soil. Nitrogen-fixing plants trap nitrogen from the air and transport it throughout the plant. Over time, their degrading roots and leaves release nitrogen into the soil in a form accessible to nearby (non-nitrogen-fixing) plants. The best types of nitrogen-fixing plants will vary by region. Common examples include clovers, lupines, and field peas. Though clovers generally prefer a higher soil pH than is tea-friendly, some varieties, like white clover, are happier than others in more acidic soil. Grasses, such as winter rye, can help prevent erosion, but may quickly overgrow and go to seed if not mowed regularly, leading to thick grass around the roots of your tea plants. Green mulches also support your garden by providing a habitat for beneficial insects or, in the case of clover and lupine, flowers for pollinators.

Whether cover crops can outcompete weeds around young tea plants may depend on how well the area has been cultivated in advance. Weeds that have gone to seed can be a long-term challenge for any gardener, but especially in a no-till garden. Many books have described approaches to weeds in permaculture gardens in great detail. Given the lifespan of the tea plant, it's worth consulting these resources. You may also want to consult guides on mulching and weed control for growing blueberries, which share many of tea's same soil requirements.

Clover mulch is not just pretty; it also feeds the bees when it flowers and contributes organic matter to the rows of tea when mowed.

Clover planted between rows of tea at Minto Island Tea Company. (The flags mark the tea plants so they don't get mowed, too!)

# SEASON-BY-SEASON TASKS

| | YEAR ONE | YEAR TWO |
|---|---|---|
| **EARLY SPRING** | Test soil, plan site | Fertilize (balanced, for example, 10-10-10) |
| **MIDSPRING** | Amend soil with compost and prepare beds | Hand-weed and apply new mulch, reseed green mulch |
| **LATE SPRING** | For fastest growth, plant seeds now through summer<br><br>Transplant one-year- to two-year-old plants, apply mulch or plant green mulch<br><br>Fertilize (balanced, for example, 10-10-10) | Hand-weed as needed and scout for pests (aphids are common)<br><br>Leave the early season growth (one to two leaves) to support the plant |
| **EARLY SUMMER** | Irrigate seeds and plants as needed | |
| **MIDSUMMER** | Irrigate regularly, hand-weed or mow as needed<br><br>Fertilize (balanced)<br><br>Cut back excessive growth if shoots are 12–18 inches, make a little tea | |
| **LATE SUMMER** | Irrigate regularly, hand-weed or mow as needed<br><br>Test soil, plan site for fall planting | Harvest a few leaves for tea |

|  | YEAR ONE | YEAR TWO |
|---|---|---|
| **EARLY FALL** | Irrigate regularly, hand-weed or mow as needed<br><br>Amend soil with compost and as needed, prepare beds if planting | Enjoy the flowers (leave them for the bees and next year's seeds) |
| **MIDFALL** | Hand-weed, reapply mulch<br><br>Transplant one- to two-year-old plants, apply mulch or plant green mulch | Collect seedpods from last year's flowers to plant or store |
| **LATE FALL** | Prepare for overwintering, apply mulch as needed to protect roots | |
| **EARLY WINTER** | Watch and wait, sip tea, take a break | |
| **MIDWINTER** | Protect from harsh weather as needed, for example, with a frost blanket | |
| **LATE WINTER** | Formative pruning if not already done | Second formative pruning |

# Growing Healthy Tea Plants (Years Three to Five)

**TEA GROWS SLOWLY** as its roots become established during the first three to five years, and it may take even longer in colder or more northerly regions. Important activities you've already performed in the first two years will continue to support your plant during this time. Starting around year three, your tea should also be ready for a little more harvesting without compromising its health. This is when the fun begins!

Weather can often have a visible impact on young plants, though this becomes less obvious as the plants mature. Although most impacts are temporary, more extreme or cumulative stress (heat, too much or too little rain, cold, nutrients, weeds, pests) may threaten the plant's survival. In summer heat especially, growing tea plants need regular moisture—because of its smaller root field, a young tea plant is especially vulnerable to drying out. You should have the capacity to water young plants and, depending on your climate, may want to irrigate regularly when weather gets hot or dry for long periods. During late winter and early spring, tea plants do not typically look their best. Their leaves can be damaged by the cold, sunburned, and sometimes frostbitten. Extremely cold weather can come close to defoliating a young or weak plant; however, most tea plants should be able to bounce back if their roots are healthy and protected from freezing.

For the first several weeks of spring, your tea plants, despite being evergreen, may look less than verdant. Leaves with frost damage may appear lighter in color, and sometimes will be crispy and burnt-looking. Older leaves, even on healthy plants, will show signs of aging and may fall off (we see this also in late summer or following prolonged heat stress). As days lengthen and temperatures rise, plants will begin to show early growth. This first flush is one of the most prized of the year. Harvesting is important—even if it's just a small amount—since this will lead to more growth. But in years three to five, especially if your plant had a rough winter, we recommend leaving some of the new growth. The plant requires leaves to collect energy, so it's important to let some stick around to do their job. When new growth is plucked, apical dominance is broken, stimulating lower shoots to grow and yielding additional new bud sets for harvest. In spring and throughout summer, new growth can continue to provide occasional leaves for harvest (so long as you don't take too many from young or stressed plants).

New growth can also provide clues to potential damage due to pests, pathogens, or deficiencies in the soil. Spots sometimes appear on young growth or young plants in times of nutritional stress, often early in the year when temperatures are cooler and root uptake is inhibited. They're usually cured by time, fertilizer, or, for plants in pots, potting up to new soil. However, diagnosing tea plants can sometimes be tricky. We recommend consulting with local agriculture advisors or camellia experts in your area if you run into trouble.

The maturing tea garden will take less work to maintain over time. Proactive hand-weeding may still be a frequent and critical effort, especially if your garden is prone to invading vines and large weeds. Mulching remains an important annual task. As discussed in the early years, an effective layer of mulch will help suppress weed growth, maintain soil moisture, and ultimately give back to the soil through decomposition over time. As plants grow larger, they also begin to provide their own shade. This can help keep soil from drying out and reduces the potential for weeds.

## FERTILIZER

Young tea plants generally don't need a lot of fertilizer, and their capacity for uptake is limited by root growth. However, fertilizer application in the early years can help promote optimal growth and guard against specific deficiencies. Because camellias are sensitive to overfertilizing, we prefer to take a conservative approach. Important roots for nutrient uptake are mostly located in the top inches of soil, radiating wide, beyond the canopy of the plant. We usually apply fertilizer broadly around the base of the plant and across the full diameter of the branches. You can apply a slow-release, balanced fertilizer in early spring, and, if desired, in late spring or early summer and midsummer. In our garden, we often skip the later applications for young plants, especially if we used a slow-release formula earlier in the season. We also sometimes use worm turnings and recommend other growers consider natural fertilizers like this as well. Because they usually have a lower concentration of nutrients, natural fertilizers are less likely to burn the plants and can help build the soil by adding micronutrients and organic matter.

In addition to nitrogen, phosphorous, and potassium, other nutrients important to tea include calcium, magnesium, sulfur, zinc, iron, manganese, and copper. On balance, calcium and magnesium interact

A healthy plant will have old leaves that fall off during spring, even while new shoots develop and the plant flourishes.

Spots on new growth can be a sign of stress.

with phosphorous, so more is not always better. Sulfur and copper deficiencies are not uncommon. Copper deficiency, in particular, may impact the ability to produce oxidized tea—it's mostly a problem in sandy soils with low organic content, but can also be a result of soil outside the ideal pH range or other nutrient imbalances. Some growers recommend using Epsom salts for a magnesium deficiency, however, the solution is often not a single factor, and you should first consider a possible excess of potassium or deficiency in nitrogen.

Absorption of nutrients by the roots is an active process, requiring energy. Therefore, plants with fewer leaves will have less capacity to absorb nutrients, and there is no need to add fertilizer directly before or after pruning.

## PRUNING

Pruning is still one of the more important activities in years three to five. While there are many reasons for pruning, they will vary over time and under different conditions. I tend to sympathize with the effort the plant has put into growing, so I usually dislike cutting back new growth. Done for the right reasons, however, pruning is good for the plant—and for the grower who wants to harvest the leaves!

In the early years, plants are pruned to help them develop as shorter, wider bushes. This is nice for harvesting, makes them stronger, and can also make them look fuller and more compact in the garden. After the major formative pruning performed in years one and two, additional pruning often continues to be necessary at least in years three and four or four and five (depending on rate of growth and when the previous cuts were made).

If a plant was not decentered early on and has a long central stem (or multiple stems), it can also be formed by pulling the vertical shoots toward the horizontal and using stakes to hold them at about 2 feet from the ground. This is called pegging. Removing the apical bud of the pegged stem(s) stimulates any new branches to grow vertically and help form the plucking table. This practice may reduce the amount of time before a plant can be harvested.

Fruit trees and decorative camellias are often trained to be low and wide using an espalier, but we've never seen the technique applied to tea. It might be worth trying, however, if you need to keep the plant close to a protective wall, have a small space, or just want to experiment with making garden art out of your tea plants. Finally, if your plant is already a tall single stalk with a few branches higher up, you may want to take a leap of faith and cut it down to size in late winter to spring. Assuming the roots are healthy, the plant should branch out below the cut.

For harvesting convenience, we recommend you maintain the height of your tea plants at no more than 3–4 feet tall. What's comfortable for harvesting will depend on your height, of course, and how many plants you are raising. When we first started making tea, we harvested from the mature plants that we also used for clonal propagation in the nursery. Our frames were taller than at a typical tea plantation, and I would develop shoulder and neck pains after only a couple hours of plucking. One year, some of our plants even grew so tall that by the end of summer I had to harvest using a ladder! You may have seen pictures of people climbing to harvest the ancient tea trees in China, but this is rather impractical for an average tea garden. I do know someone who picks tea from an overgrown tree outside their second story window, but that seems rather dangerous. To keep your tea plants from becoming trees, keep them low in early years and continue to train your plant for at least a few more years so you'll have maximum opportunity to harvest.

Kacie Merkel and Elizabeth Miller of Minto Island Tea Company in front of mature tea plants with well-formed plucking tables.

Identify previous pruning sites and the most recent cut, and look for a central dominant stem or stems (usually at least ½ inch in diameter).

Side branches (non-dominant) can be left at their original length or trimmed as desired. When plants are larger, longer side branches can be cut back as needed and lower-growing branches may be removed, especially those that reach the ground.

# WHEN TO PRUNE

We typically wait to start our pruning until mid- to late winter. This isn't *just* because we're busy or taking a break to relax over the holidays. There are a couple reasons, having to do with the plants' health. First, recovery from pruning is optimal when root starch is high. Plants undergo photosynthesis to produce energy, which helps them obtain nutrients from the soil to support new growth. When the days get shorter and colder, the plants enter dormancy, and photosynthesis drops off as enzymes become inactive in low temperatures. Energy stored in the form of starch helps prepare the plants for spring growth. Recovery from pruning takes time, and plants don't look their best after a major prune. They may start to look better by summer, but don't plan on harvesting until then.

Another reason we don't prune in early winter is to avoid stimulating plants to grow in potentially freezing weather. Plant stems harden off before winter, turning from green to a woody red-brown, which makes them better able to withstand cold. In our area, we often have unpredictable periods of warmer weather punctuated by significant freezing that can damage fragile new growth.

## MAINTENANCE PRUNE

Pruning and frame formation in a more mature plant, with branches created by earlier pruning. (Leaves omitted for clarity.)

Year three

Year one

Year two

*Before pruning*

30–36 inches

Just below plucking height

*After pruning*

# Growing Healthy Tea Plants Long Term (Year Six and Beyond)

**IN ADDITION TO HARVESTING** your tea, most of your efforts at this stage will center around managing your plant's size and (hopefully) occasional threats to its well-being. Guidelines for fertilizing older plants and dealing with nutrient issues are generally the same as for younger plants. However, additional nitrogen may be applied in spring and early summer to enhance growth for harvesting. Growth is often boosted within a few weeks of application. Therefore, we recommend avoiding additional nitrogen applications in late summer as it can cause growth sensitive to fall frost.

If you forget to pluck after a rainy week in August, you could end up with too many tall shoots like these.

With mature tea plants, the main reasons for pruning or trimming are to manage height and stimulate new growth for harvesting. Even if you aren't doing a deep prune, regular trimming can help keep things under control—growth might not be very gradual if you take time off. In early August, our plants will easily grow a foot or more if we miss a couple weeks. Plants will gradually gain height by the end of the season even if you are plucking regularly. Depending on its growth, your plant may need a medium trim to get back down to the original height of the plucking table after formative pruning. Or it may just need a light trim. Taking just a few inches off the top is useful for removing the congested "crow's feet"—when many small branches have formed on a single branch—that tend to accumulate over many rounds of plucking. The term for a light trim in the tea industry is *skiffing* (like the small flat-bottomed boat). This process helps keep your plucking table flat and low enough for the next season.

While it seems conservative to let tea plants grow on their own accord with minimal pruning, active shoots are the source of tea for plucking and these are much more abundant when the plant is forced to produce young, new growth. The first thing I suspect whenever growers mention their tea plant isn't making many shoots is that they haven't done enough cutting back, either because they don't know how or are afraid to hurt their plants. Our survey confirmed this tendency—many beginning growers hadn't pruned or trimmed their plants, including the larger ones. In fact, cutting back mature plants stimulates more vibrant, denser growth. We recommend a cycle of pruning more heavily one year, sometimes skipping a year, or following directly with lighter trimming and medium height-reduction pruning in subsequent years. Four-year to five-year cycles are sufficient, depending on the vigor of the plant.

Finally, pruning more mature plants also serves to protect or rejuvenate their health. Dead or diseased branches are a potential source of pathogens, and regular removal is a necessary aspect of preventive healthcare for tea plants. The most extreme form of pruning is rejuvenation pruning, which is meant to rejuvenate an older plant by cutting the stems as far down as several inches off the soil. Few to no leaves are left and the plant comes back from the base. In theory, early winter, when root starch is high, is the best time for any major rejuvenation pruning. As with younger plants, less-drastic trimming can be done in mid- to late winter or during midsummer to encourage later-season growth.

**ABOVE** This plant looks rather sparse just after a major prune in late winter.

**RIGHT** Within a few months, the plant is recovering.

Trimming and, especially, height-reduction pruning are my least favorite tasks in the garden. It always surprises me to see how bare the tea plants look after a major prune—sometimes it's quite distressing. Whatever growth does remain tends to look older and less attractive. These previously protected leaves are also more sensitive to sunburn, which can be a problem, especially in cold, sub-freezing weather. Although sunburn is not life-threatening for a healthy plant, you may want to take precautions by covering recently pruned plants in case of a major late winter frost. A frost blanket is ideal, as it will also reflect the bright sunshine from newly bared plants. Although they look pretty sad in early spring, pruned plants will recover using starch reserves from the roots. On recently pruned plants, spring growth may be delayed, but by midsummer, all but the most heavily pruned plants will be covered in green.

## PRUNING TIPS

### MAINTAINING HEIGHT AND PRODUCTIVITY

• Look for evidence of crowding or crow's feet.

• Identify previous pruning sites and the cut from the most recent pruning.

• For a light to medium trim, cut 3–8 inches above the last pruning. Chose a site just above a branch or strong bud pointing the direction you would like the branch to grow.

• For a major height-reducing prune, or to remove knots or congested branching, cut well below the last pruning, seeking to direct new branches when possible. For deeper cuts, be sure to let several shoots with leaves remain to help with recovery. Don't expect to harvest from this plant until midsummer.

• For a rejuvenation pruning, usually reserved for mature tea (twenty years or more) or severely infested or damaged plants, cut back stems almost to the ground. Follow frame-developing guidelines for young tea to reform the plucking table. Don't expect to harvest regularly until the plant has recovered.

I'm often asked whether or not to prune the suckers that sometimes come up at the base of a tea plant. Suckers are generally a response to stress, including pruning, drought, or damage to the plant from freezing or planting too deep. Some consider suckers to be untidy, and others suggest they take away from the growth of the main plant, but my tendency is to leave them, in large part because the plant found them important enough to generate, and therefore they must serve a purpose. Because they are young growth, they also generate pluckable shoots. I've seen examples of tea camellias even spreading by suckering, though I haven't observed it in our garden (at least not that I know of—it's hard to differentiate suckers from the volunteer seedlings that crop up under mature plants).

**ABOVE** New growth will emerge even from the larger branches after a hard or rejuvenation prune.

**RIGHT** When you want to have the plant put on more growth, let a full shoot grow before harvesting. Note the pruning site at the base and plucking site atop the shoot.

A strong primary trunk with root suckers (here a response after the plant was blown over in a storm)—leave them if you like or cut them if they're crowded.

# SEASON-BY-SEASON TASKS

| | YEARS THREE TO FIVE | YEARS SIX TO TEN AND BEYOND |
|---|---|---|
| **EARLY SPRING** | Fertilize (balanced, for example, 10-10-10) | |
| **MIDSPRING** | Hand-weed and apply new mulch; reseed green mulch | |
| **LATE SPRING** | Irrigate and hand-weed as needed; scout for pests<br>Fertilize (balanced) | |
| | Harvest a few leaves if the plant has overwintered well | Harvest regularly starting with first flush |
| **EARLY SUMMER** | Irrigate, hand-weed, and mow as needed; scout for pests | |
| | Regular light harvest if growth is vigorous | Harvest regularly |
| **MIDSUMMER** | Irrigate, hand-weed, and mow as needed; scout for pests<br>Optional: prune to reduce height if you aren't regularly plucking | |
| | Harvest lightly, or regularly if growth is vigorous<br>Fertilize (balanced) | Harvest regularly<br>Apply nitrogen-rich fertilizer if harvesting regularly |

| | YEARS THREE TO FIVE | YEARS SIX TO TEN AND BEYOND |
|---|---|---|
| **LATE SUMMER** | Hand-weed and mow as needed; scout for pests | |
| | Harvest lightly, or regularly if growth is vigorous | Harvest regularly |
| **EARLY FALL** | Enjoy the flowers (leave them for the bees and next year's seeds) | |
| **MIDFALL** | Collect seedpods from last year's flowers to plant or store | |
| **LATE FALL** | Prepare for overwintering, apply mulch as needed to protect roots | |
| **EARLY WINTER** | Watch and wait, sip tea, and take a break | |
| **MIDWINTER** | Protect from harsh weather as needed, for example, with a frost blanket | |
| **LATE WINTER** | Additional formative pruning | Occasional heavy pruning |

# Threats and Pests

Certain pests and environmental threats can prevent your plants from thriving. In our experience, poor drainage and overwatering are the biggest threats to tea plant health. Before treating for anything else, check soil pH and drainage—high pH and soggy roots will both compromise nutrient uptake even if your soil doesn't have any actual deficiencies. If you haven't already done so, apply a balanced, complete fertilizer suited for acid-loving plants (such as Holly-tone).

Just as we caution against overwatering, we also advise against letting your growing plant dry out, especially in hot weather (you don't need to water in winter when plants are dormant). Your plant will tell you in no uncertain terms if you have failed to water enough. Leaves will turn brown and crispy; if too many of them do this, the plant won't survive.

If your plant dries out too much in hot weather, the leaves may turn brown, especially at the tips. Recovery and new growth is possible with watering.

# YELLOW LEAVES

There are many causes of yellowing in tea leaves and they can range from harmless to deadly.

- Older leaves may appear yellow and die early in the growing season. This is a normal part of the lifecycle of the plant.

- When the leaves of an entire branch suddenly turn yellow (and then brown), it is likely due to fungal infection and requires timely removal of the branch.

- Uniform yellowing, poor growth, and wilting, especially in heavy, wet soils, may signal root rot—roots will be brown instead of white—which requires removal.

- Sunburn is caused when leaves are exposed to an increased amount of light, as when shade is removed suddenly. Though unsightly, it's not terribly harmful if the plant is otherwise healthy.

- The leaves of tea plants can experience winter stress like other camellias; in temperate climates this is often due to a combination of exposure to cold, sun, and wind.

- A lack of nitrogen can lead to chlorosis (the inability to produce enough chlorophyll), which causes uniformly yellow leaves. Nitrogen can be added back in spring or summer.

- Micronutrient deficiencies, such as iron deficiency, may lead to yellowing between the veins (interveinal chlorosis). Before adding micronutrients, make sure the underlying problem is not soil pH.

- Cold stress during leaf-bud development may also manifest in growth weeks later with yellow along the outside margins.

- Yellow spots are a sign of scale, usually on lower branches. The underside of the leaf will show white spots and sometimes a cottony appearance if the infestation is extensive.

Signs of developmental stress on growing leaves during an early spring cold spell in an Oregon tea garden.

# PESTS

Tea pests (for example, insects) and pathogens aren't common in North America and the British Isles. While there is a broad range of diseases that can affect tea worldwide, many are a concern primarily in tropical regions and areas where tea is grown as a commercial monocrop. When tea is grown in a large concentration, it is possible for pest problems to develop that wouldn't be as apparent in a home garden or setting where tea has never been grown previously.

However, it's well known that ornamental camellias can be impacted by a range of garden-variety pests and pathogens. The same solutions generally apply to tea camellias, with the important exception that most people prefer not to spray chemicals on the leaves of tea intended for human consumption.

If kept to a minimum, most pests aren't fatal to the mature tea plant, but a severe infestation can threaten the health of younger or stressed plants. Here we describe just a few of the most common examples and highlight other potential pathogens.

**Aphids** may be an issue in greenhouses and on young plants, especially. They suck on the sap of growing tea buds, young leaves, and stems, which leads to curling and stunting of new growth. Luckily, they're not terribly harmful and can be removed physically by rubbing them off or by spraying with diluted dish soap or horticultural oil (just don't plan on harvesting the sprayed shoot).

**Tea scale** is a common problem on ornamental camellias and also on tea. It's caused by sucking insects underneath the leaf and manifests as yellow spots on the leaf's top side. While the insects are very small and hard to see, they often have a characteristic powdery

Ants like to farm aphids on new growth. Heavy infestations can be wiped off with a tissue—but watch out for fire ants if you live in the South!

or fluffy white covering. Scale often starts on inner or lower leaves, so it can be hard to spot infestations until they have progressed. It can be treated by fully saturating the underside of leaves with horticultural or neem oil. As plants mature, an adequate flow of air under and around the plants can reduce the burden of scale. For this reason alone, it's worthwhile to prune lower branches and promote airflow.

**Mites** can be a seasonal problem. For example, southern red spider mite can be a problem in the southeastern United States in spring and fall. Broad mite, or yellow tea mite, is a widespread greenhouse pathogen found on all sorts of crops. Broad mites cause a plant to secrete growth hormone, leading to deformed new growth and scarring on the underside of mature leaves. These mites can be difficult to eradicate—horticultural or neem oil can help, but because the mites concentrate in newly growing shoots, using oil can pose a challenge if you plan to harvest. In our garden, we see signs of broad mites primarily in early spring and fall; their activity is reduced by high heat. Routine pruning of new growth can reduce infestations.

**Chilli thrips** are invasive pests from Asia that are spreading across global agricultural regions. They feed on leaves, buds, and tender plant stems with piercing-sucking mouthparts, which can lead to discolored new growth and leave a cork-like scarring on the backs of leaves. Their preference for new growth also leads to deformed leaves. While thrips typically don't kill their host plant, an infestation can compromise new growth.

**Root-knot nematodes** are roundworms that live in and around roots, sometimes creating galls and generally inhibiting function and leading to stunting and failure to thrive. They're mostly a problem for young plants. With heavy infestations, remediation may include removal of the plant and replacement of the soil.

Certain beetles, weevils, caterpillars, moths, and butterflies will also eat tea. Though generally not a problem, some may yield devastating results—for example, newly planted rows of tea can be decimated by certain types of armyworms. Other common pests, like the Japanese beetle, an invasive species in North America that eats over 200 types of plants, seem to leave tea alone or feed only incidentally if there isn't anything else to eat.

Not all pest pressure is harmful. For example, leafhoppers induce a certain kind of metabolic stress that spurs leaves to create chemicals responsible for the uniquely delicious flavor profile and aromas in "bug-bitten tea."

On a much larger scale, herbivores are sometimes a concern with tea, though less so than with many other plants. Tea plants are

Tea scale appears as yellow spots on the top side of the leaf; a heavy infestation will turn the underside of the leaf white—at this point it is best to remove the leaves.

Broad mite infestations lead to interesting new leaf forms, such as curling and fused.

Long-term mite damage will cause deformed, corky leaf undersides and less healthy plants.

somewhat deer resistant due to bitter tastes imparted by caffeine and catechins. Our experience is that tea is not their first choice—but no plant is immune from a hungry deer. They are most life-threatening for young (one- to two-year-old) tea plants and less of an issue for larger or mature plantings. Unfortunately, deer are rampant in many residential areas where wild forage is not readily available. Tall fencing, at least 8 feet high, can be effective, and small cages surrounding younger plants may help protect them until they're large enough to withstand a few nibbles.

All leafhoppers are welcome in our garden as long as the plants are healthy!

# INFECTIONS

Though blister blight (*Exobasidium vexans*) is an important fungal pathogen of tea worldwide, it's not yet known to be a problem for tea in the United States or United Kingdom. Problems with blister blight seem to be greatest in cool, moist environments. Anthracnose is another blight, caused by fungus, that affects many plants including tea. Canker and dieback due to fungal infection affects camellias in hot and humid environments such as the southeastern United States.

We have rarely seen serious fungal infections in our tea garden, with the exception of the ubiquitous soil pathogens that can cause root rot. High organic content in the soil leads to a relative abundance of fungi or bacteria that feed on dead or decaying organic matter. Root rot, due to excess moisture and growth of the fungus *Phytophthora*, is probably one of the worst problems experienced by new growers because it can lead to total decimation of the plant. By the time you know it's happening it has probably progressed too far to fix.

Symptoms of root rot can include yellowing or browning of leaves, defoliation, twig and branch dieback, and ultimately the death of the plant. Initial symptoms, such as wilting, can be subtle and hard to distinguish from the effects of heat or drought. You can identify root rot by looking at the color of roots underground—living healthy roots will be white. *Phytophthora* may naturally exist in the soil and slowly incubate until symptoms suddenly appear. Rot can often be traced to poor drainage, and it can spread among plants. Unfortunately, since fungi can remain in the soil even after you remove affected plants, completely replacing the soil or relocating plants may be necessary. We recommend you don't directly replant in a site where you suspect root rot has occurred, or at least wait a year or two or bring in new soil.

Other potential pathogens include honey fungus, which is mostly a problem in the British Isles, and sudden oak death, which is presently spreading in the western United States. Honey fungus is a fungal infection under the soil, characterized by rotting roots and a white fungus between bark and wood. Occasionally, honey-colored mushrooms appear at the base of the plant. As its name suggests, sudden oak death, caused by an infection with *Phytophthora ramorum*, is responsible for widespread destruction of oaks in parts of Northern California and Oregon. Camellias are also an affected host. Infections typically start at tips of the leaves and lead to defoliation over time. Unfortunately, this condition is difficult to differentiate from other fungal damage and can only be confirmed through laboratory tests.

# HOW TO TREAT A SICK-LOOKING PLANT

Prevention is often the key to success. Unfortunately, chemical or physical treatments to eradicate pests may also reduce their insect predators and create a cycle of susceptibility to repeat infestation. We use horticultural oil and sometimes neem oil for treating problems in our greenhouses. We don't tend to use them in the garden because problems are rarely as bad. Beneficial insects can also be a solution, such as introducing lady bugs to eradicate aphids. There are plenty of practical and philosophical reasons for choosing to use or not use pesticides. We prefer nature's balance whenever possible.

Soil mycorrhizae, those beneficial symbiotic fungi, are also part of a healthy garden ecosystem. While experiments show that inoculation of nursery plants with arbuscular mycorrhizae fungi helps with nutrient uptake, this practice is not yet commonplace for tea plants. These fungi may grow naturally in forested or undisturbed soils, which could explain why some tea industry books recommend planting on undisturbed or cleared forest land.

If pest issues are impacting new growth midseason, you can trim back the plants as you might for a light or medium prune. If you have widespread infestation, this will help lessen the impact without using chemical products and may also reduce a reservoir of infection, since many pests, though inactive, will persist in the crevices of the youngest growth. If you do plan to spray something, pruning or trimming can also reduce the treatment area and increase access to some of the older leaves.

For issues impacting more mature growth, pruning will also remove diseased branches. Cut below the damage to reduce the chance of spreading. If damage is widespread, rejuvenation pruning is an option—assuming you have healthy roots, the plant will often grow back from the base.

If the entire plant is suffering and doesn't improve with treatment, or if you suspect root rot, we recommend removing the plant entirely. Digging out the plant is relatively easy, but leaving feeder roots in the ground may contribute to the persistence of the fungal infection in the soil. Ideally, dig up the soil, add compost, and plant with a cover crop—or at least don't put another camellia in that location for a few years. If you have an ongoing problem, consult an expert in your area, as pathogens and best practices vary depending on local climates and soils.

# Growing Tea in Pots and Other Special Circum- stances

Many people drink tea with a passion and are excited by the prospect of growing their own. We totally understand—there are so many reasons to grow your own tea, not the least of which is the desire to get to know the plant we love to drink! Others, when they learn where tea comes from, may want to experiment with tea in their garden or add to their efforts to grow their own food. Over the years we have met many tea growers from a variety of backgrounds. Not everyone has a garden; some just want to try a plant or two, and some live in a climate less suitable to tea, with cold winter weather or hot and dry summers. Given the right infrastructure and care, tea can grow in many different environments, surviving and sometimes even thriving in conditions outside its typical climate. That said, tea is not a houseplant, and we don't recommend starting a tea farm in the high desert or in an alpine meadow. However, where there's a will, there is often a way—in this case, there are many ways to extend or adapt a tea-growing environment in a wide variety of situations.

# Growing Tea in Pots

These plants (aged 1, 2, and 3 years) have been regularly fertilized and moved to larger pots each year.

**WE HAVE INTRODUCED** you to the various ways of starting tea in pots, so here we'll cover a longer-term project and prospects for *keeping* tea in pots. Of all the reasons for wanting to grow tea in pots, there is only one wrong one. Many people have the impression that tea is a tropical plant and assume incorrectly that it can easily be grown indoors. In fact, while tea does grow in warmer parts of the world, it is completely unsuited to the warm, dry indoor air we enjoy in our temperature-controlled homes.

We want to emphasize that *tea plants will rarely thrive indoors*— they may not even survive unless their need for sufficient light and lower temperatures are met. All camellias, including tea, prefer a period of dormancy, and winter temperatures below 60°F are optimal. They also need a lot of light to survive indoors; for example, from a bright south-facing window or artificial lights. During frost-free times of year, tea plants should be taken outdoors; though if a plant has been indoors for more than a few days, changes should be made gradually, starting in a shaded location.

On the other hand, it's quite possible to grow tea in pots outdoors for ease of care, occasionally bringing them indoors to protect them from harsh winter weather (with attention to coolness, water, and light, of course). Growing tea in pots can be a good solution when soil or available space outdoors are insufficient, if plant predators such as deer or voles are a problem, or for gardeners who want to focus on planting only natives in the ground and keeping their tea "contained." Low outdoor temperatures are fine; mature leaves will tolerate hard frosts, and assuming the plants are healthy overall, they will usually survive if the roots don't freeze. Plants in pots have the same basic needs to flourish as those planted out in the garden or field, but conditions like frost protection and convenient watering are easier to control.

## GUIDELINES FOR GROWING IN POTS

No tea varieties have been specifically selected for growing in pots. We recommend choosing whatever type is suited to the outdoor climate in your area; for example, if you expect freezing temperatures, choose cold-tolerant varieties. If you want to experiment with more tender varieties, pots can be an excellent choice, allowing you to occasionally move the plants to an indoor space when they might otherwise not survive winter. We personally find that many of the tender plants in our collection can still flourish outdoors once they're mature, so long as their roots are healthy and they have enough foliage to tolerate some loss. Young plants, on the other hand, do well in a cool greenhouse.

Plants in pots grow equally well from seed or from cuttings. However, the advantages of a taproot are lost when plants are kept in pots, so there's no need to use a deep pot to accommodate one. The taproot will curl around the bottom of the pot, but it will die if it is damaged during transplanting or dries out in a root-pruning pot. In fact, some people believe cutting the taproot to increase branching provides a better root system for pot-grown camellias.

The same principles of suitable potting soil apply to starting tea and to growing plants long term—tea plants don't like their roots to stay wet, so a well-draining mixture is essential. We recommend composted pine bark, which can be combined with various additives, such as sand or perlite. Most commercial potting soils are sufficient, but be sure they are acidic. If in doubt, look for something labeled as an azalea or camellia mix. Peat moss is okay to use if you're concerned about the plant drying out—though take care, as peat moss compresses easily, and you could end up using too much. If in doubt, use less. It's especially important to balance peat with drainage, as too much moisture held in the soil will eventually rot the roots. We only use peat moss in seed mixtures, preferring to water our potted plants more frequently.

Repotting is a great way to care for your tea plant and stimulate growth. This can be done as often as once per year, or every two to three years as plants mature. The choice of pot size is important. Tea plants should be started in smaller pots, so they use up the water in the soil between waterings. Using too large of a pot compared to the plant's roots can result in the soil staying too moist. Conversely, if plants are left in smaller pots, or go for longer without potting up, they may become root-bound. When repotting, gently loosen the roots and, if needed, cut any roots that are tightly circling the pot. Remember, the taproot is not an advantage in pots so don't be afraid to cut it.

A slow-release, balanced fertilizer or common liquid fertilizer can be used as directed. Cottonseed meal or worm compost are favorites for organic production. Fish or blood meal can help if leaves are yellow, but unless you're harvesting with regularity, additional nitrogen isn't usually necessary. Fertilize plants first thing in spring and when repotting. Don't fertilize plants when they are dry—water first! In hotter climates, do this in the evening when temperatures are below 90˚F.

Despite their need for well-drained soil, tea plants in pots shouldn't dry out completely. Depending on ambient temperature and humidity, plants in pots may need watering more frequently than they would in the ground. A good rule of thumb is to water often enough so the soil is still somewhat moist within a quarter inch of the surface. Always ensure excess water can drain out and don't keep the pot in a tray of water for long.

A partially shaded deck or patio provides a good home for moderately sized tea plants in pots. Afternoon shade is especially helpful in warmer climates. In colder climates, just as with plants in the ground,

This Sochi tea plant self-seeds in its pot—these volunteers can be shared with friends and neighbors.

## POTS IN PRACTICE

### An experiment indoors

Several years ago, I started a casual experiment, raising a tea plant from seed at home. Knowing that tea doesn't like warm, dry air in winter, I brought my plant into the bathroom next to a south-facing window where it would routinely receive steam from the shower. It survived winter. The next year, I kept it in a glass porch. This location provided much better light and was cooler than the house. It was also easier to bring the plant outside whenever we ran into a stretch of comfortable winter weather. I rarely fertilized except when potting up every one to two years. Going on five years now, the plant is much smaller than it would be in the garden.

My experimental indoor-outdoor seedling is surviving but not thriving—here, its growth at four years is similar to that of a two-year-old seedling grown outside.

## Tea on the back deck

Angela McDonald of Oregon Tea Traders in Eugene, Oregon, is starting her own tea from seeds and self-propagated clones in pots on her back deck. Her mild Willamette Valley weather poses less of a challenge than do migrating deer. Her setup is ideal as it provides protection from marauding herbivores and easy access for monitoring and caring for the potted plants both in summer and winter.

## Tea on the patio

Reserving his garden for natives, tea lover and experienced gardener Michael Pratt has grown tea in pots for several years. In a temperate region of northern Alabama, these var. *sinensis* plants thrive outside year-round, withstanding winter temperatures as low as 15°F. Mike believes his plants are successful because they're situated on an east-facing side of the house, protected from the afternoon summer heat that ranges from 95°F to 100°F. Starting with two-year-old plants in 1- to 3-gallon containers, he pots them up every few years and fertilizes regularly throughout the growing season. Now in 22-inch pots, the prospect of repotting becomes more daunting!

Angela's pots of young tea are easy to care for close to the house.

Occasionally harvested for tea, but not regularly pruned, Mike's beautiful specimen of yellow tea spreads vigorously. At this point, it's 8 feet wide.

be cautious about exposure to morning sun in winter. The nice thing about pots is they can be moved to meet these needs.

How you manage your larger plant depends on your long-term plans. If you're looking to harvest, you should prune to promote the development of a frame with as many branches as possible. If you want to grow your tea in a pot indefinitely, then your goal is similar to tending a bonsai—you must create conditions that allow for a long and healthy life in a container. Tea wants to grow into a small tree, and if your plant is growing well, you will eventually need to cut it back. Keep in mind that larger plants are more challenging to repot; additional midseason pruning can help keep plants small. Though this may temporarily reduce your harvest (depending on how much you prune), repotting will yield a vigorous plant with more tips to harvest in the subsequent year. Eventually, you can limit the growth of your mature potted plants by trimming their roots.

We usually start our tea in pots as cuttings or transfer them to pots as seedlings. We keep them in greenhouses for one or two years before planting them out in the garden or selling them to customers. The greenhouses are covered with shade cloth in summer and can be closed in winter when weather gets below freezing. We pot up the plants into larger containers with new soil and fertilize and water regularly. They do well under these conditions.

The greatest danger to growing plants in pots outdoors is having the roots freeze, which irreparably damages the plants. If tea plants become defoliated due to freezing, they will usually come back if the roots are healthy. However, if the roots are killed, the plant won't have the resources to recover—even while the plant maintains its leaves (for example, if you protect the foliage but not the roots). Our potted plants at Camellia Forest aren't allowed to go for long periods of sub-freezing temperatures. Generally, we heat the greenhouses minimally when temperatures go below 30°F, and we push the pots close together to protect the roots. But if temperatures get much colder (we routinely go below 20°F and sometimes below 10°F), we layer the plants with frost blankets as well. Frost blankets alone will protect the plants for a short time below 30°F, but we recommend adding heat or bringing them indoors when temperatures fall below 25°F. Growers with outdoor plants can provide additional protection by pushing pots together and covering them with leaf mulch or needles. Snow will also insulate the plants from deep freezes, which in our area routinely follow the occasional snow and ice storm.

# Growing Tea in Shade or Among Trees

**THOUGH TEA IS OFTEN** grown in full sun for production purposes, some US tea growers are leaning into its heritage as an understory plant, developing "forest tea gardens" and installing their tea under existing trees. These include growers on Hawaii's Big Island, others in the foothills of the Blue Ridge Mountains, and the folks at Table Rock Tea Company, who are planting under South Carolina's pines.

Eliah Halpenny and Cam Muir have grown tea on Hawaii's Big Island since 2001. Their goal is to "re-create the environment that tea evolved in." Near 3,000 feet elevation, in a temperate zone that supports other crops like lettuce, Big Island Tea grows in a deliberately designed Hawaiian cloud forest with native trees such as ohia and kukui. They also plant among koa, which are leguminous and put nitrogen back in the soil. A scientist, Muir's specialty is ecological genetics, studying how organisms evolve in various environments. Muir and Halpenny maintain that forest-grown tea provides an ideal chemistry, since the diversity of bacteria and fungus species in the soil creates a wild and thriving forest that nurtures and flavors tea plants (and anything else grown there). Understanding the relationship between soil microbes and tea cultivars holds a potentially promising key to developing climate-specific strains of tea plants.

Cam and Eliah in Big Island Tea's cloud forest.

A row of Big Island Tea bushes among ohia and other native Hawaiian plants.

**ABOVE** These Big Island Tea plants are flourishing under their kukui canopy.

**RIGHT** Pine trees shelter these tea plants from strong afternoon sun at Camellia Forest.

Growers without a forest of their own may decide to selectively plant companion trees to provide shelter or shade that can reduce the impact of wind, cold, or intense sunshine. Evergreen pine trees or other conifers are particularly useful for shelter and protection from winter sun. We grow our var. *assamica* and other tender tea relatives under pine woods and cedar trees. Shorter evergreen shrubs pruned into a protective hedge can work well as a windbreak, but keep in mind their demands for water if you're growing in a drier climate. In some settings, roots from larger trees and shrubs can compete with your tea plants for limited water. This is what we expected; however, in our most recent plot, after the first year, the young tea plants grown closest to the pine trees were larger and more robust than those in full sun. Maybe the protective benefits from the trees outweighed any competition for water and nutrients. In the end, after a full growing season, the difference was less pronounced. It may take years before we know the true cost/benefit of proximity to the pines.

Our younger plants (three years old) get smaller the farther away they are from trees and would probably appreciate some afternoon shade.

# Growing Tea in Colder Climates

**GROWING CAMELLIAS** in colder regions is the topic of William L. Ackerman's excellent book *Beyond the Camellia Belt* (2007), and the principles are generally similar for tea. Gardeners face several challenges growing tea in colder and more northerly regions. Responding to shorter day length in northern climates, tea plants will start to grow later in spring and stop sooner in fall. This shorter season may limit potential yield—plants may survive as a unique specimen in a casual personal garden but are less likely to thrive for production purposes without greater effort. In colder climates, planting tea from seed (rather than clones) sourced from cold-hardy varieties may provide resilience, due to their genetics and taproot.

In some regions, protection from the cold is the key determinant of whether plants will survive. Winter sun can be particularly damaging. "Sunburn" often follows frost early or late in the growing season. Reasons for this aren't well documented. One possibility is that freezing temperatures cause the leaves to wilt and desiccate, making them vulnerable to damage from UV radiation.

To reduce the likelihood of scorching, plants can be situated to avoid morning sunshine, for example, along a wall, hedge, or line of evergreen trees. In our garden, we protect our most tender tea plants (the var. *assamica* types) under a line of cedar trees just north of a small grove of pine trees. A friend recently reported success growing a couple small-leaf varieties in the Delaware Valley near Philadelphia; the plants are situated at the base of pine trees as protection from winter sun.

Tea plants may defoliate from episodes of severe cold, but if the roots aren't frozen and were healthy to start, the plants can often recover. Planting in a sunny south-facing space may create a microclimate with warmer soil temperature in the summer. Black plastic or landscape fabric can also help increase soil temperature—just make sure it doesn't cook the roots underneath (we suggest limiting this as a temporary measure in lower-light situations). There's also less solar radiation at higher latitudes, so you might want to use white or aluminum reflective mulch to increase the amount of light available for photosynthesis.

These apparently contradictory options (protecting from winter sun and planting to increase southern exposure, or use of black plastic versus white mulch) are impractical in large-scale production, but aren't insurmountable for the determined home gardener. Another option is to grow under hoop houses. One of Camellia Forest's customers, Light of Day Organics, grows their tea under a double-walled greenhouse in Michigan! Temporary protection, such as frost blankets, are especially useful when winter weather is unpredictable.

Last, but not least, you should also have a plan to protect your tea in case of heavy snow. While moderate amounts of snow can actually help protect plants from the cold, especially when accompanied by dry air and bright sunshine, the accumulation of heavy snow and ice can break limbs. Proper forming of the tea frame through pruning develops a strong network of branches that's better able to bear the weight of wet snow or ice. A hoop house may help if you expect major winter weather on a regular basis. But even hoop houses can collapse under snow if the design is not sufficiently strong. A structurally sound greenhouse will provide both protection from severe cold and snow damage.

Properly formed frames allow these tea plants at Westholme Tea Company to support a heavy blanket of snow.

Stone raised beds and plastic surrounds provide Tulloch Tea's plants with individual protection.

## ENGLAND AND SCOTLAND

Despite long days in June, tea grows slowly at northern latitudes, reducing the number of harvests in a season. But growers as far north as Scotland are finding that the leaf produces a high-quality tea. Protective measures, including surrounding plantings with trees and the use of polymer ground covers and plastic tunnels, can help plants withstand winds and chilly, cloudy weather.

In many parts of Scotland, the Gulf Stream helps create a mild climate in which frosts are few but winter gale-force winds are common. New growers at the Isle of Lismore Teas, situated on the west coast of Scotland, use low shelterbelts to provide windbreaks. Growers at Guisachan Tea in the Scottish Highlands planted their tea in a fenced garden, using wooden cold frames to help get them started. Also in the Highlands, since 2017 Tulloch Tea has situated their 1,500 plants on an acre of south-facing ground, using miniature raised beds made from stone for each individual plant. This keeps the temperature of the soil around the roots slightly warmer. Their young plants produce just enough leaf to use in cosmetics and blended tea.

# Hot and Dry Climates

**TEA GROWS BEST** with rainfall evenly spaced throughout the growing season—a far cry from Mediterranean climates seen in the western United States or the hot summers of central Texas! However, aspiring tea gardeners in warm climates will be heartened to note that many locations where tea flourishes still need occasional watering to get through dry periods. These include otherwise hospitable areas such as South Carolina's Wadmalaw Island, home to the Charleston Tea Plantation, and Oregon's Willamette Valley, which supports Minto Island Tea Company. Internationally, tea also grows in oasis settings such as in northwest China's Gansu Province, a former waystation along the Silk Road, and Shaanxi Province, where the dry, windy season often brings sandstorms. Coastal regions of Iran and Turkey are also good examples of microclimates—here, the ocean's influence provides suitable areas for tea in countries best known for arid interiors.

Minto Island Tea Company's young plants have irrigation from the Willamette River to get them through Oregon's dry season.

Irrigation is a must for starting tea and developing strong roots in hot and dry climates. As in colder climates, plants grown from seed can develop a taproot, which may provide resilience. Even in areas with more rainfall, such as coastal regions of Northern California, Oregon, or Washington, hot and dry periods still occur during summer months. In these and other dry climates, we recommend an active program of substantial and regular irrigation throughout summer. Minto Island Tea Company is a great model—they water their young tea plants via overhead sprinklers connected to the Willamette River. Your plants' supplemental water needs may increase with higher temperatures, which often lead to greater evaporation. If you have limited access to water, heavy mulching can reduce evaporation.

As temperatures rise during the day, humidity typically decreases, and at very low humidity, tea plants will stop growing. At around 95°F, photosynthesis also begins to decline. Planting in areas with midday or afternoon shade is an effective way of reducing leaf temperature in hotter and dryer climates. Growing in pots can also be handy, allowing you to move the plants to follow the shade (but keep in mind that pots can dry out quickly so require careful attention to watering).

## CALIFORNIA

California is a perfect example of an area that is quite dissimilar from where tea evolved. Yet, despite the classic Californian Mediterranean climate (i.e., wet, but relatively warm winters and warm to hot and dry summers), camellias are grown extensively throughout Northern and Southern California coastal regions, and even some inland regions such as Sacramento, home to one of the oldest camellia shows in the United States. Tea is one of the many camellias also grown at Southern California's Descanso Gardens, north of Los Angeles.

According to agronomists at the University of California, Davis, working at the Global Tea Initiative and the nearby Kearney Agricultural Research and Extension Center, several locations along the California coast and throughout the Central Valley have potential for tea farming. Researchers at the Kearney institute are studying a decades-old collection of tea plants left after a Lipton-funded research project ended in the 1970s. These and other longstanding California-grown cultivars may prove important sources of plant material for regional gardeners in the future. Scientists are studying how the specific cultivars interact with soil microbes, nitrogen, and water availability to affect growth and qualities of tea. One question is whether heat stress can favorably impact tea quality, perhaps depending on the timing of irrigation relative to harvest. Lessons learned from establishing California as an agricultural leader in both wine and blueberry production bode well for tea's long-term prospects.

## HAWAII

The state of Hawaii features a number of examples of nature-adapted tea planted under unusual conditions. Depending on their location, growers face unique challenges. Volcano Winery, located on the dry side of the Big Island, must protect their plants from "vog," a mixture of fog and volcanic ash that, depending on the wind direction, blows through their land. However, they found that their wine infused with tea leaves was so popular that sales justified growing their own crop. On the other side of the island, tea growers on former pineapple or sugarcane lands face a challenge from sea-blown salt deposited on growing leaves, which impacts the processed tea's flavor.

Numerous efforts seek to establish a Hawaiian tea industry nurtured by the islands' distinct terroir of soil and climate. Regional branding distinguishes the precise geography of a plant's cultivation, for example, "Volcano" or "Kilauea." Some growers use techniques originated elsewhere, such as Japanese-style matcha, but Hawaiian-grown leaves give the familiar preparation a distinctive flavor. State university research and development efforts have produced several unique cultivars to fit Hawaiian conditions, and the College of Tropical Agriculture and Human Resources will soon release a new cultivar to the public, continuing their practice of improving and differentiating Hawaiian strains.

Johnny's Garden, established in 1993, is Hawaii's oldest tea location still in operation. Around two dozen locations currently grow Hawaiian tea. Most of Hawaii's tea farms are less than five acres.

Volcano Winery's popular wine infused with black tea, both grown on their site.

# Growing Tea in a Changing Climate

**AS CLIMATE CHANGE** brings more weather extremes, adaptation is something we all need to think about. Small differences in temperature may extend the range in which tea can be grown without a greenhouse. On the other hand, many areas may experience lengthy droughts, heat waves, and an overabundance of rain and flooding. We might need to extend practices used to protect tea in cold or hot climates to a wider range to help prepare for these types of weather events. Tea growers in Africa, from Rwanda and Kenya to Malawi and Zimbabwe, are already having to adapt to longer, hotter, and drier weather conditions. Some will have to shift cultivation to more suitable climates.

As we have emphasized, drainage is very important for successful tea growing. With climate change, some areas may experience greater amounts of year-round rain, which could strain the drainage capacity of existing soil. In the case of one unlucky tea grower north of Seattle, flooded fields ultimately killed a substantial number of their plants. Erosion due to extreme heavy rain is also a concern; tea planted on a slope may be more vulnerable to erosion and flooding.

Several practices meant to protect growers from extreme weather events are likely to create a favorable environment for tea even under ordinary circumstances. For example, we've discussed how planting from seed increases resilience, as the deeper root growth that results is more resistant to drought and cold. Planting among trees is another good example, as forest shades tea plants, absorbs runoff from heavy rain, and (if evergreen) shelters plants in cold weather. There is no more "normal" when it comes to climate and growers of all stripes must learn to adapt. Luckily, the tea-growing community is full of enthusiastic innovators already hard at work thinking up and testing new methods to help tea thrive.

# Harvesting and Processing

In ancient times, tea was considered a medicine. Medicine doesn't usually taste great, and raw tea leaves are no exception! Fresh, unprocessed tea leaves impart limited flavor to water. The vast majority of flavors and aromas we enjoy in tea were discovered over centuries of experimentation with different processing methods.

Just as drinking tea is an art with centuries of tradition across many cultures, the methods for processing slowly evolved as traditional craft through trial and error, both occasionally leading to new discoveries. Most processing in the modern tea industry is highly mechanized. At the same time, scientists and industry experts are trying to uncover new clues that could lead to better practices. Home growers can learn the basic principles of tea processing and adapt them for small-scale production; the endeavor provides ample opportunity for lifelong learning.

When starting to grow tea, you'll have several opportunities to harvest leaf or use materials from pruned branches during the early years, but regular harvesting should wait until your tea plants are at least three to five years old. The wait may last even longer in cold or northern climates or in other situations with slow growth. Once tea plants are established and healthy, they will be a reliable source of increasing amounts of leaf that can be harvested every two weeks or so during the growing season.

**TWO OF THE MOST** common challenges for new growers are a lack of information on processing techniques and limited plant materials. Many beginners make the mistakes of underpruning and underplucking, which limit new growth throughout the season. As long as your plant is healthy, pruning and plucking will increase the vigor of leaf production in the months and years ahead. While a mature plant can yield as much as one pound of processed tea per year, you can still enjoy the smaller yield available during early years, harvesting small amounts of leaf once or twice per season.

Let your young shoots grow at least one or two full leaves before plucking them. Each harvest stimulates new shoots, so you can continue this practice at intervals throughout the growing season as your plant develops. My rule of thumb is that a small handful of shoots (about six sets of the standard "two leaves and a bud") will make enough dried tea for a six-ounce cup. This amount can provide immediate gratification, or you can save it until you have enough to fill a tea pot.

The processing steps outlined in this book are guidelines based on my own experiences, scientific studies, and all that I've learned from various teachers and books about best practices. They've been modified as needed to meet the requirements of smaller-scale production, and there's plenty of room for creative adaptations. All the processes described here can be carried out by everyday gardeners using inexpensive equipment you may already have in your kitchen.

Artisanal tea production is both a craft and an art, perfected over the course of hundreds of years and across different cultures. The craft is knowing the basic steps and conditions, which this book supplies. The art is developed by the practitioner with experience—as you become familiar with the feel, sights, and smells of the process, sensing how to adjust the timing of each step, your own art will develop. My personal journey with tea is one of lifelong learning, especially when it comes to working with the leaf. There will always be more to learn about best practices, discovered and honed over centuries to produce the teas that consumers know and love. But fresh tea is also delicious, and there is plenty of opportunity for anyone to learn the craft and develop their art through practice, personal experiments, and creativity.

Tea shoots, stimulated to grow after the last pluck, are green and ready to be plucked again.

# Harvesting

**HARVESTING TEA CAN** be a wonderful experience. Hand plucking is precise and peaceful. For me, it's a quiet time that lends itself to meditation and creative musing. Even when interrupted by the sound of the neighbor's lawn mower or radio, I find it relaxing. Is it the aroma that rises from the plants as they warm in the sun? Some say it reminds them of cannabis—maybe I've subconsciously made a connection. More likely it's the anticipation of later aromas that arise during and after processing, which I consider the high point of the experience. Plucking can be a timeless, focused activity. It can help to have a meditative state of mind, songs to sing, or a friend to share the task.

Though tea plants require three to five years of growth before significant harvesting can take place, we encourage growers to take advantage of summer pruning opportunities in the early years to harvest a few leaves. This will stimulate branching and you may be able to harvest several cycles of increasing amounts of leaf. Remember to leave enough new growth to support photosynthesis as well as allow the plant to increase height and branching.

Latitude and temperature will determine the start of the growing season and the first flush of growth. In temperate regions, tea is dormant in winter when day length falls below eleven hours for six or more weeks. In spring, in addition to longer days, nighttime temperatures need to be above 50°F for at least a few days. This allows soil temperatures to equilibrate and stimulates the plants to break dormancy. We've noticed some plants start later than others in our garden. Those tend to be cultivars more adapted to northern climates, such as Japan or Korea. I have come to appreciate this difference as it reduces the risk of a late frost damaging tender new growth.

A tea plant's "first flush" of new growth is treasured (for green tea especially) because of the flavors that become concentrated in the leaves during winter dormancy. Normally, a tea shoot will follow a predictable growth pattern. The first couple leaves are small and not used for tea, but they are soon followed by up to five new leaves before the terminal bud. In spring's cooler temperatures, growth is slower. Approaching summer, plants will grow more vigorously and you'll soon be able to harvest the next flush. Plants will continuously produce new growth about every two weeks, depending on the weather.

# HOW TO PLUCK

A growing shoot will typically start with a small leaf that's not usually harvested—called the "fish leaf." This is followed by the first mature leaf, the "mother leaf," then up to four to six leaves before terminating in a dormant (or terminal) bud. *Banjhi* is a term that means dormant and can be used to define an entire tea plant or the bud at the end of the growing shoot. I've also heard it used for plants that have reached maturity and need a major prune to stimulate growth. You can harvest leaves from this growing shoot at various stages. Removing the apical bud and some leaves stimulates lower buds to create new growing shoots that you'll be able to harvest as they mature.

All the basic plucks for making tea are made on new growth, which is characterized by green, tender stems that are easy to snap or cut with your fingernails. Snapping is easiest and basically involves grasping the stem between your thumb and forefinger and gently bending it until it breaks. When harvesting by hand, it becomes apparent when older growth shouldn't be plucked. If the stem is too tough to pluck easily, it's probably too tough to process by hand. You could use pruning shears, but they can make it harder to notice this toughness, and you'll end up with tough, overly mature leaves that

A terminal leaf bud (banjhi) is dormant and no longer growing.

Two leaves and a bud make the standard pluck—and a handful of leaves makes a small cup of tea!

must be sorted and separated from your final tea product (this is especially noticeable in oxidized teas). Plucking below the fish leaf isn't going to kill the plant, but it gives you more stem in your processed tea and could potentially reduce the plant's productivity in the subsequent year. In young plants, we recommend plucking above the first mature leaf.

"Two leaves and a bud" is the standard pluck for high-quality tea. In this method, you remove the most terminal unopened leaf bud at the very top of the new shoot, along with the next two open leaves. The fine pluck preferred for white tea is only one leaf and a bud, or sometimes just the unopened bud for a very fine pluck. Note that a fine pluck works best on varieties with very large buds—we often use the buds from our larger-leaf var. *sinensis* cultivar, which are about twice as large as most other shoots. Specific Chinese cultivars have been selected over time for traditional white teas like silver needle tea. A coarser pluck is suitable for oolong or black teas. This includes the third and sometimes even fourth leaf. Oolong tea can be made when the terminal leaf bud is fully developed. Some growers will harvest larger growing shoots and later separate out the top two leaves and bud for green tea, saving the lower leaves for black or oolong. This method can provide a more uniform response to the conditions and manipulations needed to process the leaf.

After plucking, gently place your leaves in a basket or bag. At this stage, you want to keep them from overheating, drying out in the sun, or being bruised, as these stresses impact the chemical processes in the leaf and how it responds to further processing. Avoid plucking on a rainy day or very early in the morning when the leaves are wet from dew. If leaves are wet and you must harvest, you can gently blot them dry them with a towel or let them air dry in the shade. Never move them into the sun to dry as they can burn very quickly! Occasionally, I have to rinse our tea leaves to remove visible deposits of the pine tree pollen that drifts through our area for a few weeks every spring. In these instances, I use a salad spinner with a basket to rinse and gently spin them to remove excess water.

## WHEN TO PLUCK—TIME OF YEAR

Harvesting can begin in spring when the plant starts growing. For us this can be as early as mid-April, depending on weather. Plants will start to grow earlier if they're in a greenhouse, but the most important determinant is day length. As days get longer and plants start to grow, care must be taken to anticipate and avoid the impact of late-spring frosts. The new leaves of a first flush are exceptionally tender and susceptible to frost damage. In North Carolina, we have a good amount of temperature variability in March and April, so there have been times when the tea has started to grow and I've had to rush to harvest what I could before a sudden frost.

In my garden, I often do a fine pluck early during the first flush. A fine pluck is also a good choice when harvesting from a young plant or one that's recovering from winter pruning because it leaves more new growth on the plant to support its energy needs. Patience is key—the plants will grow faster in summer and more harvest will be possible in the weeks and months to come.

With longer days, warmer temperatures, and sufficient rain or irrigation, growth will accelerate, and you may need to harvest as often as every seven to ten days throughout summer. Some of my well-established plants will put on a foot or more of growth in just a couple weeks. In those instances, the stems tend to be less developed and a coarse pluck is not only easier but also necessary for height management. If the weather is very dry, growth may be delayed, only to resume or even accelerate after a wet spell. In extended dry periods (two to three weeks or longer in summer), I sometimes irrigate to stimulate growth. In late summer, and early fall, the plants begin to flower

## PLUCK TYPES

A tea shoot showing new growth and plucking points for different types of tea.

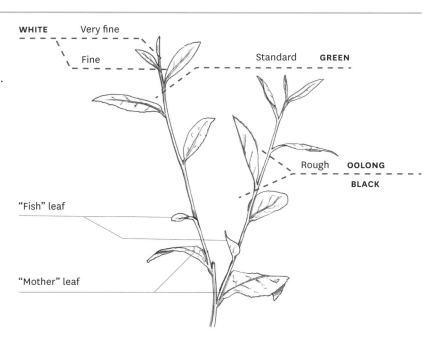

WHITE — Very fine

Fine

Standard — GREEN

Rough — OOLONG

BLACK

"Fish" leaf

"Mother" leaf

and leaf growth slows considerably, but leaves can still be harvested. If you're growing in a colder climate, be sure to allow your plants sufficient time to harden off (when stems mature and turn from green to brown, going from tender to tough) before the first frost.

## WHEN TO PLUCK—TIME OF DAY

Plants respond to sunlight, humidity, and temperature—the flavors and textures of your tea leaves may change a little throughout the day, but I've never been able to tell a major difference in taste depending on the time of day a leaf is harvested. I usually end up plucking to suit my schedule, avoiding rain and midday summer sun, and considering the processing needs for individual tea types. Importantly, when you pluck will have an influence on the conditions for subsequent processing steps. For green and white tea, I tend to pluck early in the day. For oolong, late morning or early afternoon is fine, but not later, since the leaves need to undergo a "sun wither" when the sun is still high in the sky. I don't like to harvest when the weather is very hot and sunny, as the leaves sometimes become limp on the plant (which could compromise the withering process). Harvesting in midafternoon is okay for black tea, but not later in the day when the leaves become tougher as their pores close to conserve water.

# Processing

**WHILE TEA PROCESSING** may be considered an "artful craft," it can also be approached as a science. If you're so inclined, you can measure, record, and attempt to control all the various parameters. It's a bit like cooking—understanding the science, or at least some of the general principles underlying the craft and art is helpful. But a degree in chemistry or vast technical knowledge and specialized tools aren't necessary to succeed. Everyone can have fun and enjoy the process of making tea in whatever style they prefer.

# OXIDATION

Tea types are most often grouped by degree or type of oxidation. Oxidation is the technical term for the chemical processes that turn tea leaves from green to brown. In some ways, it is similar to what happens when a cut apple starts turning brown on the surface after being exposed to air. Oxidation creates variations across different types of tea; green tea is the least oxidized, while black tea is fully oxidized. There are some exceptions, such as first-flush Darjeeling, which is a lightly oxidized "black" tea with a very short oxidation time. Oolong teas have a wide range of oxidation, from almost green (*pouchong*) to almost black. Green tea processing uses heat to stop oxidation before rolling (see page 149), while black and oolong teas include various steps to assist oxidation. In white tea, oxidation is allowed to occur at a slow pace without any assistance.

Oxidation occurs when enzymes within the tea leaf interact with oxygen to create specific chemical changes. Polyphenol oxidase is one of the most important enzymes in tea—it's responsible for the chemical reactions that transform catechins into theaflavins and thearubigins, which give black tea its distinctive taste. Rolling the leaf helps break down the cell walls to allow mixing of the polyphenol oxidase enzyme with other cell contents. The functional activity of polyphenol oxidase is sensitive to temperature—levels increase steadily between 60°F and 80°F then decrease at higher temperatures, until the enzyme is no longer functional above about 165°F.

Sometimes (especially in historical texts) the process of oxidizing tea is called fermentation, but fermentation is technically a different process, a chemical breakdown of a substance by bacteria, yeast, or other microorganisms. In Chinese tea culture, "black tea" is a term used for fermented tea (pu'erh), while in the West, the vast majority of teas consumed as black tea (called "red tea" in Chinese) are oxidized and not fermented.

# EQUIPMENT

Whether on a large or small scale, the same principles apply to processing specific types of tea. However, working with smaller batches requires flexibility. Smaller quantities of leaf require less time for heating and drying. Rolling techniques must also be adapted. For example, you can roll individual leaves or small handfuls in a small cotton napkin or directly by hand.

A simple electric wok with a bamboo steamer rack and lid are all you need to make green tea.

Kitchen equipment that most of us have at home (or can easily buy) is useful for small-batch processing in the main steps of withering, heating, rolling, oxidation, and drying. Keep in mind that tea leaves will take up the scents and flavors of other foods, so it's important to use clean or dedicated equipment unless you like the idea of garlic-, onion-, or fish-scented tea (or whatever strong-smelling foods you may like to cook). In my kitchen, the oven isn't used for much besides tea (occasionally cookies) during the six-month-long tea-processing season. For smaller quantities, a toaster oven is a great option, but look for models that include lower heat settings (180°F or lower). A convection feature is useful but not required. Some home growers have mentioned using a microwave to dry tea and others use a dehydrator; however, heat settings on dehydrators are typically too low, and while home microwaves may be able to dry tea to a crisp, they lack the easy temperature-control features of a regular home oven. Because drying temperatures are important in creating specific qualities in finished tea, and also because proper drying is critical if you are planning to store the leaf, we recommend using a reliable oven.

Other handy items, though not necessary, offer a greater level of control over certain aspects of processing. These include a digital scale (one that measures grams or tenths of ounces) and possibly a handheld infrared monitor (with an adjustable emissions setting) to gauge the surface temperature of things like woks or frying pans. Although I've never used it, one grower mentioned using a seed heating mat to assist in oxidizing black tea.

## WITHERING

Withering starts immediately after harvest and is an essential step leading to key physical and chemical changes. Tea can be placed in a tray or basket in the shade or indoors, preferably in a relatively cool environment (68°F–80°F). This step lasts between two and twenty-four hours for most types of tea, with a target of 20–50 percent moisture loss by weight. Physical withering can be measured by weighing the tea before and after withering—calculate the percent change by dividing the post-withered weight by the pre-withered weight. For example, if you start with 100 grams of fresh leaf, you will expect to achieve post-withering weight of 50–80 grams. During withering, the leaves become soft and pliable to the touch. Held upright by the stem, the withered leaf should collapse into a C shape.

# EQUIPMENT FOR TEA PROCESSING

| STEP | EQUIPMENT | SMALL BATCH ADAPTATIONS |
|---|---|---|
| WITHERING | Large basket, tray, mesh rack | Small basket, soil or flour sifter, pie pan, paper towel on a plate |
| HEATING | Temperature-controlled wok, steamer insert, table-top steamer | Small stainless-steel pan or pot, steamer basket |
| ROLLING | Lint-free flour sack towels, laundry board | Lint-free napkins, sushi rolling mat |
| OXIDATION | Same as withering, or a bread proofer if you live in a dry environment | Homemade "proofer" with humidifier, or oven and pan of water (experiment using a thermometer with humidity detection to find what works best with your equipment and environment) |
| DRYING | Kitchen stove oven, ideally convection | Toaster oven, ideally with low-temperature settings and convection |

After physical withering, the leaf is soft and can form a sideways C shape.

### SUN WITHERING

After plucking for oolong, sun exposure increases the production of many aromatics, similar to those induced by insect damage or other stressors. The precursors to aromatics vary by cultivar, so some types of plants may be more responsive to this process. Longer is not better, and extended exposure to intense sun may lead to scorching.

In addition to physical changes in the leaf, important chemical changes (i.e., chemical withering) take place during this time. These changes greatly influence the flavors and aromas of tea, reducing astringency and increasing aromatics. Lower ambient temperatures allow chemical withering to progress, and it typically takes longer than physical withering. The length of time leaves need to wither will vary depending on the type of tea you're making, with shorter times for green teas, longer for oolong and black, and longest for white tea. Oolong is the only tea that requires sun withering.

Temperature and humidity during withering play an important role in how quickly leaves lose moisture—higher temperatures may lead to premature physical withering, or even hardening (when the outer casing of the leaf dries before the interior of the leaf has become dehydrated). If you're processing in a dry climate, including indoor, air-conditioned environments, you may want to experiment by creating a closed space where you can maintain a higher humidity level to achieve a longer chemical wither. A homemade humidity chamber can be a device like a bread proofer, or a simple setup like a towel draped as a tent or a large box placed over the tea and a pan of water on a hot pad set to low (with of room for the tea to breathe).

## HEATING

Heating plays an important role in creating all types of tea, with different effects at different stages of processing. For green and oolong teas, heating the leaf is a critical step used to stop oxidation before rolling. This is sometimes called "kill green" (*shāqīng*) or "fixation," because moderate to high temperatures (at least 165°F–180°F) deactivate polyphenol oxidase, the enzyme that promotes oxidation. Final drying also includes sufficient heat to further inactivate polyphenol oxidase. Depending on the type of tea, more or less heat is used during final drying. Higher heat contributes to flavor changes and additional browning. For this reason, much lower temperatures (for example, in a dehydrator or with shade-dried tea) won't yield the flavor range expected of most traditional teas.

# ROLLING

Rolling is a very important activity in processing most types of tea (with the exception of white tea). It entails applying firm pressure to break down cell membranes and release moisture from the leaf. This moisture release allows sufficient drying—in black tea it's also necessary to promote sufficient oxidation. If leaves for green tea are dried directly after the kill-green step, without rolling, the dried product will be considerably heavier. Rolling may also affect taste, since releasing juices during rolling makes them more accessible once the leaves are infused in water.

Insufficient rolling is sometimes a problem when beginners start making tea, as most people don't realize how much force and time is required—especially with manual processing. Machines are useful for managing the rigors of rolling larger quantities of tea, but none are designed for the small or even micro-batches of leaf that most beginners will be processing. The guidelines below are for a home grower who might have several mature plants to harvest, yielding sufficient amounts of leaf to warrant rolling in a cloth napkin or small towel.

To hand roll, gather the leaves into a lint-free cloth, creating a ball, and twisting the cloth to secure (we use 24-inch-square flour sack towels, which can be cut into quarters for processing smaller batches). With the palm of your hand, begin kneading the ball in one direction, pressing firmly against a clean surface. Some people recommend using an old-fashioned washing board (or a sushi mat for smaller amounts), as the ridges may provide additional traction. After a few minutes, open the cloth and gently separate the leaves before drawing them back into the ball and repeating the rolling action in the same direction. Continue to roll and repeat; over time (five to ten minutes), the leaves should begin producing moisture through the cloth. (Note that the juices will stain whatever they touch, including your hands, with prolonged contact.) Strong rolling should continue, and moisture should become more visible (or even drip) on the surface. Continue the process of rolling and separating for up to thirty minutes, while reabsorbing any expressed moisture into the cloth to coat the leaves.

It can be difficult to knead or roll small amounts of leaves. One effective method is to carefully roll them between your two palms. I've also used a small silicone tube (marketed for peeling garlic) to roll a small batch wrapped in cloth. Another method that yields quick results is placing the leaves in a sandwich baggie or similar plastic and using a rolling pin to gently apply pressure until the leaves express moisture. For tough leaves (as for black tea), a brief freeze before rolling can help break down the leaf structure without as much physical work. However, thawed leaves require extra care, as they break apart easily. I've found the plastic-bag-and-rolling-pin method is enough for most leaves.

**ABOVE** Tea is gathered in a cloth to make a tight ball for rolling.

**ABOVE RIGHT** Inside the cloth, the soft leaves will begin to stick together.

**RIGHT** Roll, break apart, roll, and repeat, until the juices are released.

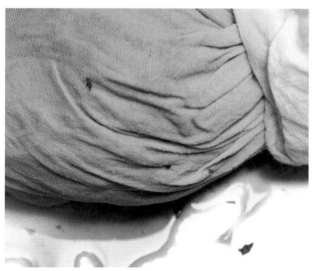

## DRYING

Drying with heat is the final step. Heat stops any further oxidation and, especially at higher temperatures, helps create additional aromas and flavors through the Maillard reaction. The ideal temperature for drying varies by the type of tea. It can range from lower temperatures (180°F) for white and green tea, to higher temperatures for oolong and black teas (220°F). These aren't hard-and-fast rules. For example, oolong processing can use different drying temperatures to achieve different outcomes—indeed, the process of roasting previously dried oolong tea is an art in itself (some oolong teas are modified years after they are produced); specially designed home roasters are made for this exact purpose. Drying also removes moisture from the leaf so it stores well.

## EVALUATION AND STORAGE

If you have enough leaf and a precise scale, weighing is a good method to determine whether your tea is sufficiently dry for storage. Dry tea should weigh about one fifth of its original weight at harvest. For smaller batches, another way to determine if your tea is dry enough is whether it feels crispy in your fingers (or mouth).

After making and drying your tea, you can store it for several months or longer. Containers should be airtight and kept in a dark space. When I was working with very small amounts of leaf, I bought small food-grade tins to store individual batches. I like to store my white and green teas for no more than twelve months, as the most unique and delicious fresh aromas of these teas tend to diminish with time.

Freshly processed tea is delicious, but tea flavors and aromas also mature over time in storage. Even though the leaves are dried, there is still some moisture remaining in the cells, so chemical and non-chemical oxidation does take place. Several home growers, myself included, have noted the more oxidized teas especially tend to age well—often tasting better after being in storage several months.

### THE MAILLARD REACTION

The Maillard reaction converts sugars and amino acids (the building blocks of proteins) into a variety of chemicals, including some that contribute to browning as well as others that produce a range of aromas. Some of these are easy to recognize as flavors we often enjoy in tea (for example, nutty, toasty, or honey-like), while others seem a little distant from what we'd expect (meaty, garlicky, or putrid). The Maillard reaction is usually seen in cooking processes involving heat, where it optimally occurs at around 280°F–320°F (higher temperatures result in caramelization, a different process). This reaction can also occur at lower temperatures, especially in the presence of water. The small amount of water remaining in tea leaves after processing combined with the Maillard reaction contributes to changes in tea aromas during long-term storage.

# Main Types of Tea

## WHITE

In China, white tea is usually made from special types of *Camellia sinensis* characterized by fine white hairs on their large, unopened buds and on the undersides of their youngest leaves. Grown in specific regions, such as Fujian Province, and harvested early in spring, their common names include "white hair silver needle," "silver needle," and "white peony" tea. Whether white tea is a specific process or a cultivar depends on who you talk to—there are certainly cultivars especially well suited to making white tea, but here we are focused on the process.

Making white tea is a great introduction to the aromas and tastes of fresh tea and a perfect place to start making your own tea at home, especially when you have only a small amount of leaf. White tea is the simplest tea to make. It can be considered unprocessed since it only involves a very long wither, undisturbed in the shade or indoors, followed by an optional drying. The conditions for withering, however, play an important role in the quality of the finished tea. Ambient temperatures and humidity should be moderate.

As the tea leaves slowly wither, chemical reactions create changes in various aromatics over time. It can be fun to follow this process with your nose—though it may be harder to sense these differences in very small batches, you can concentrate the aroma by holding the tea cupped in your hands. When the leaves first begin to wither, they produce a fresh, almost floral smell. After twenty-four hours they exude a somewhat unpleasant aroma (to me, it smells a bit like old fish). This effect comes from one of the chemicals that later dissipates as it is further transformed. If you plan to store your tea, you must dry it, but white tea is really most delicious in the first few months. It has a unique sweetness compared to more processed teas.

Fine white hairs on the leaf bud and young growth lend a silvery sheen to withering leaves.

Dried, the leaves have a dark, semi-oxidized look, and the hairs are obvious against the darker background.

# *How to Make White Tea*

**HARVEST** Use a fine or very fine pluck (one leaf and a bud, or just the bud), preferably in the morning.

**WITHER** Remove to a shady site (or inside) and spread on a cookie sheet, tray, or basket at moderate temperature (68°F–80°F) and higher humidity (>65 percent). Leave for twenty-four to forty-eight hours undisturbed.

**DRY** Use a low temperature, 180°F in an oven, twenty to thirty minutes, or until dry. A lower temperature is okay if you wish to use a dehydrator and don't plan to store the tea long.

**DRINK** Infuse white tea at 185°F, five to six minutes. The infusion will be pale, and tastes will be nutty, sometimes grassy, with a sweet aftertaste.

An infusion of white tea and tea flowers.

# GREEN

The most important step in the making of green tea is the deactivation of enzymes that transform color and flavor in other types of tea. The goal is to render the enzymes inactive while preserving the integrity of the leaf—this requires bringing the leaf to at least 165°F for sufficient time to disable polyphenol oxidase. Because enzymes are concentrated in new growth, processing younger leaves may require more time and higher heat than processing older leaves. The time needed to deactivate the enzymes also depends on the heating method and the amount of leaf. Smaller amounts of leaf and methods involving high heat, such as steam or using the microwave, may require a shorter time—as little as fifteen to thirty seconds! Heated leaf should be bright green rather than olive or yellowish, which is a sign of overheating.

The two most accessible methods for heating leaf are dry pan firing and steaming. I prefer pan firing because I can sense the temperature more easily when I handle the leaves and I'm able to more finely monitor progress. Steaming may be somewhat more efficient and tends to yield a greener finished product and bolder, "fishier" flavor if done properly. However, it can be a little trickier to judge when steamed leaf has gone far enough since the steam can obscure your view or burn your hand. Other modern methods that use common kitchen technology include heating leaves in a microwave or a *sous vide*. Microwave time depends on the volume of leaf and the machine's wattage, and I find it can be easy to overcook the leaves. A *sous vide* provides a precisely controlled temperature environment and may be worth trying if you enjoy playing with technology.

# *How to Make Green Tea*

**HARVEST** Use a standard pluck, preferably in the morning or midday.

**WITHER** Remove to a shady site (or inside) and spread on a cookie sheet, tray, or basket. Let sit four to eight hours at 68°F–80°F. For steaming, shorter times are okay because the physical softening of the leaf is less important (even no withering at all can work—though steaming time may need to be adjusted); for pan-fired tea, longer times are recommended.

**HEAT** There are two main methods to stop oxidation: pan firing or steaming.

For pan firing, leaves are placed directly in the hot wok and can be stirred and turned by hand or using a brush or soft spatula.

> **PAN FIRE** in a clean, dry wok or pan using medium heat (around 250°F). A handheld infrared thermometer is useful for monitoring temperature and ensuring exact conditions. Use a clean spatula or your hands to gently and constantly mix and turn leaves as they heat. Feel the leaves get hot, then somewhat sticky (three to five minutes, depending on leaf quantity). Hotter temps increase the risk of scorch, but temperatures that are too cool won't be effective and may encourage oxidation.

> **STEAM** in a tray or basket over boiling water with a closed lid. Steam for fifteen to sixty seconds or until leaves turn bright green. You may need less time if you're only steaming a few leaves. If you go too long, the leaves will begin cooking—so take care. Use caution with steam, since it can burn you.

> A less common method is to **MICROWAVE** the leaves in a small container at fifteen- to thirty-second intervals, stirring two to four times to redistribute the leaf for even heating.

For steaming, place leaves on rack, heat the pan to 350°F or more, add ½ cup water, and cover.

Whatever method you use, when you're finished, immediately turn the leaves onto a lint-free cloth and spread to cool. You can use a cold ice bath for faster cooling (as you'd do for parboiling), carefully draining and blotting to remove excess moisture.

**ROLL** After the leaves have cooled, gather them into a cloth and twist it into a ball. Place against a clean surface and begin rolling with the palm of your hand, pressing the ball and moving toward the twist. Every few minutes, open the cloth and break up the ball of leaves. Repeat until leaves are compact and sticky and moisture seeps through the cloth. Steamed leaves will wet the cloth very quickly, but still require force to expel moisture from the leaves. If leaves have been oversteamed, they may break apart with pressure. Continue rolling, repeatedly unpacking and rewrapping and rolling the leaves until liquid flows freely (you should be able to squeeze it out through the cloth).

Steaming too long will discolor the leaves and make them too delicate to roll without damaging.

**DRY** Open the cloth, break apart the leaves, and place them on a clean pan in a drying oven. Dry on low, 185°F–200°F. A wok at lower temperatures can also be used to dry the leaves. After tea is sufficiently dry (based on weight or texture), store in an airtight container away from light and heat.

**DRINK** Infuse green tea at 140°F–185°F (for steamed green tea use temperatures below 165°F) two to six minutes or to taste. If the water is too hot or the tea infused for too long, the leaves may produce a strong, even bitter, taste. Pan firing tea will create a "toasty" flavor and yellow/golden infusion, while steaming may yield a "fishy" taste and greener infusion.

# OOLONG

Oolong teas can be characterized as having a wide range of oxidation—anywhere from 10 to 90 percent. One of the things that sets oolong tea apart from green tea is that the pluck includes three or four mature leaves. You can pluck this configuration when the full shoot has developed up to five leaves and the terminal dormant bud has appeared. I sometimes find it hard to capture this moment. Because an immature leaf bud is likely to oxidize more quickly than all the other leaves, you could also pluck the first one or two leaves and a bud for green or white tea and save the mature leaves for oolong.

Another feature unique to oolong is that withering includes sun exposure for the first thirty to sixty minutes (though to avoid scorching, light shading may be needed if the sun is very strong). This solar withering is followed by hours at cooler temperatures (68°F–80°F) with an occasional agitation of the leaves through shaking. For larger amounts of tea, hand stirring or tossing the leaves is the easiest method. For smaller amounts, we've used a salad spinner turned sideways, rotating it slowly to allow the leaves to be tossed. This period of withering is key to aroma creation and may go on for several hours. It's marked by a gradual oxidation along the veins and edges of the leaf. Since these processes are so varied, we encourage you to experiment. Shorter times will create more of a greenish oolong with floral or fruity aromas, while longer times may result in richer, smokier flavors.

After the desired level of withering has been completed, oolong teas are pan fired to stop further oxidation. This is followed directly by two or three rounds of rolling, using less pressure than you would for green or black tea. In those teas, more pressure in rolling causes the leaf to distribute more juice—using less pressure keeps the juice inside the leaf and is what allows oolong teas to be infused more than once. You can also add flavors with additional roasting or pan firing after withering and the first fixation. Many stages in the making of oolong require an expert sensing of aromas before proceeding, so it's not really possible to simply follow standard timing and steps. I don't expect to become an expert oolong maker in this lifetime, but I enjoy practicing.

Leaves are withered briefly in the sunshine, but not so long that they burn.

**ABOVE** Gentle shaking starts the process of oxidation in sun-withered leaves. Here, shaken leaves are on the left, unshaken withered leaves are on the right (they are starting to dry out because they are very small and the weather is hot).

**OPPOSITE** Different degrees of oxidation in oolong will yield various shades, aromas, and flavors.

# How to Make Oolong

**HARVEST** On a sunny day, preferably by midmorning, pick the leaves using a coarse pluck, including the terminal dormant bud if available. Depending on the age of the stem and how fast it's growing, you can get more of the larger leaves. If you have to tear or cut the leaves off the bush, then they are too mature to process easily by hand.

**SUN WITHER** Place on tray or cloth in a sunny site, thirty to sixty minutes. Stir leaves occasionally to distribute exposure to sun and monitor for heating. The amount of time may be longer (up to two hours) on a very cloudy day.

**INDOOR WITHER** Remove to a shady site (or inside) to wither in a basket or tray at 68°F–80°F, at higher humidity (over 65 percent). Shake or stir every sixty minutes for six to eight hours until red veins and edges show and aroma begins to ripen. Take care in warm temperatures or dry air to ensure the leaves don't dry out.

**HEAT** Pan fire similar to green tea to stop further oxidation. Importantly, the many variations of oolong are created through differences in the degree of firing and additional oxidation. For a light oolong (greenish), try pan firing followed by rolling without further firing. For darker oolongs, you can repeat pan firing after rolling and increase the temperature.

**ROLL** After the leaves are soft enough to roll without breaking, gather them in a lint-free cloth, and roll as for green tea. Repeat this process until the leaves are compacted and sticky. Depending on the degree of firing you used, the leaves may not drip.

**DRY** In an oven, dry at a medium temperature, 220°F–250°F, for twenty minutes, then lower to 180°F–200°F until dry. When the leaf is crispy, or about 20 percent of its original weight at harvest, it's dry enough for storage. Store in a cool space in an airtight container and away from light. Sometimes oolong teas are roasted after spending time in storage, refreshing older teas and contributing to depth of taste and aroma.

**DRINK** Infuse oolong tea at 185°F–195°F for three to five minutes. Reinfuse as desired and note the changes in flavor and aroma. Tastes will depend on the degree of oxidation, roasting, and drying temperature.

# BLACK

Although black tea is the most widely consumed tea today, the process for making it is relatively new, having only developed in the sixteenth century in China. As its popularity increased and the British started growing tea in India and other countries, methods were developed to enable higher levels of production at lower cost through mechanizing key steps such as rolling. Modern developments include a "cut-tear-curl" method, which increases efficiency, yielding small processed leaf pieces. While much of the tea produced for mass consumption in tea bags is harvested and processed by machine, hand processing is still the most practical method for small-scale production, especially for the home grower. Teas produced by the cut-tear-curl method often have different flavors from whole-leaf teas made through orthodox methods, including more of certain polyphenols, greater soluble matter, and brighter color. Hand-rolled black teas tend to be more aromatic and lighter in taste and color than typical tea-bag tea.

Withering is an extremely important step for black tea. Physical withering can occur in a relatively short time (for example, six hours), so lower temperatures (68°F–80°F) are necessary to slow this part of the process and allow the chemical withering time to progress. This step can even include a period of storage. After withering, leaves must be rolled with a firm hand until the juices flow, similar to green tea processing. The characteristic colors and aromas of black tea are formed after rolling, through oxidation of the polyphenols. Polyphenol oxidase acts in concert with oxygen to transform catechins: theaflavins are formed earlier in oxidation and contribute a yellow-orange color, while thearubigins accumulate with longer oxidation and contribute a darker color. Together, they contribute the characteristic color of black tea leaf and the infused drink.

During oxidation for black tea, leaves begin to turn coppery red.

# How to Make Black Tea

**HARVEST** Pick leaves using a standard or coarse pluck, anytime between morning and midafternoon. If you have to tear or cut the leaves off the bush, then they are too mature to process by hand. Depending on the age of the stem and how fast it's growing, you can get more of the larger leaves.

**WITHER** Remove to a shady site (or inside) to wither in a basket or tray at moderate temperature (68°F–80°F) and humidity (55 to 65 percent). Let sit twelve to eighteen hours, until leaves are soft and very pliable.

**ROLL** After the leaves are soft enough to roll without breaking, roll them as for green or oolong, to the point that moisture seeps through the towel and onto the surface.

**OXIDATION** Open the cloth, break apart the leaves, and place them in a clean pan or basket. Let sit, in the shade or indoors, two to eight hours or until they turn reddish brown. Stir occasionally to allow air to circulate. Some people recommend oxidation at a lower temperature (65°F–75°F), but at warmer temperatures oxidation will go faster—many teas are made in warmer climates with higher temperatures and short oxidation times. It's important to make sure your leaves don't dry out until they have fully oxidized, or the surface will harden, preventing oxygen from entering.

**DRY** Once the leaves have sufficiently oxidized, dry them in an oven at medium temperature (220°F–250°F), ten to fifteen minutes, then decrease to 180°F–200°F until dry. Use a lower temperature for smaller amounts of tea. Tea will be dry when it's crispy, or about 20 percent of its original weight at harvest. Once dry, store in an airtight container in a cool space away from light.

**DRINK** Infuse black tea in just-boiled water, three to five minutes. Tastes may vary depending on the pluck or type of leaf, degree of oxidation, and drying temperature.

# QUICK REFERENCE FOR PROCESSING

|  | PLUCK | WITHERING |
|---|---|---|
| **WHITE** | Very fine to fine | Indoors or in covered shade, 48–72 hours |
| **GREEN, OPTION 1** | Standard | Indoors, 6–12 hours |
| **GREEN, OPTION 2** | Standard | Indoors, 1–6 hours |
| **OOLONG** | Standard to coarse | Sun, 30 minutes<br>Then indoors, 6–12 hours shaking or stirring |
| **BLACK** | Standard to coarse | Indoors, 12–24 hours |

**PLUCKING:** Pick leaves for white, green, and oolong in the morning or before noon—avoid plucking late in the day as leaves will be tougher. Very fine = bud only, or one leaf and a bud; fine = two leaves and a bud; coarse = bud plus two to four leaves.

**WITHERING:** Leaves will lose moisture and chemical changes will begin. Oxidation is limited after longer time periods and increases after disruption of the leaf, as in oolongs. Leaf will become pliable and soft. For oolong, leaves will begin to show red around the edges and veins.

**HEAT INACTIVATION:** For green tea, the leaves will become brighter and limp. Pan-fired leaves also begin to feel sticky. Other methods can include using a sous vide (to 185°F) or a microwave (use care to not cook the leaves!).

| HEAT INACTIVATION | ROLLING | OXIDATION | DRYING |
|---|---|---|---|
| None | None | Unassisted | Low (180°F) |
| Pan firing in a clean, dry pan | Yes | None | Low (185°F–200°F) |
| Steam for 15–60 seconds | Yes | None | Low (185°F–200°F) |
| Pan firing, same as for green<br>Repeat after rolling, 2–3 times | Yes | Variable | Medium (220°F–250°F) for 20 min, followed by Low (180°F–200°F) |
| None | Yes | 2–8 hours | Medium (220°F–250°F) |

**ROLLING:** Use a small, lint- and scent-free cloth for ease of handling. For all teas, rolling must be firm. For green and black teas, continue rolling until juices are released; this helps remove more moisture from the leaf for green tea, and for black tea, aids oxidation.

**OXIDATION:** Spread leaves up to a few inches deep in a tray or basket until they turn reddish-brown. Warmer temperatures lead to shorter oxidation times.

**DRYING:** The time required for drying depends on many factors, including the degree of moisture loss from withering and pan firing and success at rolling. Final weight of dried leaves should be about 20 percent of weight of raw leaves. Sufficiently dry leaves will be crispy.

You can add a delicate, smoky pine scent to nearly dry tea by heating pine needles under your wok's steamer basket. Cover and monitor to ensure the needles don't burn.

A traditional form of storing tea adds a delicious citrus aroma.

# Other Types of Tea

**THE WORLD OF TEA** processing is vast, extending well beyond the pages of this chapter. Processed tea offers endless possibilities for crafting and blending. Other teas include "yellow tea" or pouchong (a very lightly oxidized oolong), matcha (the powdered green tea traditionally used in Japan and produced by whipping powdered leaf with boiling water), fermented pu'erh, and stem tea.

Stem tea is a favorite of mine and a simple way to use long stems left over after plucking vigorous growth. After pinching off leaves, toast the stems in a dry pan—you may hear a slight popping sound. Dry and store as for other tea types. Brewed as for green tea (185°F), stem tea tastes nutty and sweet. Its caffeine levels are lower than tea brewed from leaf.

The final drying steps of tea processing may also include scenting tea with various aromatic woods or needles. For example, I used my wok on a low setting (about 200°F) to heat pine needles under the steamer basket holding nearly finished dry tea. Covering the wok with its lid for about thirty minutes effectively pine-smoked the tea, which was delicious. A little goes a long way though—carefully monitor time and temperature, and adjust to taste.

Even after tea is fully processed and dried, it can be manipulated and flavored. Traditional tea-stuffed mandarins impart a delicious flavor to made tea. We frequently enjoy this orange-scented beverage at Camellia Forest.

In Morocco, sweet green tea steeped with fresh spearmint is a traditional drink (though Moroccan mint is a named ingredient in several dried commercial tea blends, it is simply spearmint). The green tea is prepared first, then the fresh mint is added, boiled, and sweetened. Other herbs can be used, including aromatics such as sage, thyme, verbena, and wormwood. Sugar is traditional, but optional to taste. Most recipes specify using gunpowder tea, which is strong-flavored and astringent, providing a nice balance with the mint. A delicious, cold, and simplified version of traditionally prepared Moroccan mint tea involves simply adding fresh mint leaves to a carafe filled with ice and pouring over with a robust green tea brewed at double strength.

There is plenty of exploring to do as you begin learning more about the ranges of aromas and flavors produced from the tea leaf. While perfection is a worthy goal, we encourage growers to learn from their experiences. If you're seeking to emulate a particular type of tea, research and specialized efforts may be needed, especially if your environment doesn't fit the profile of the place where that type is traditionally grown and processed. For me, honing my personal tea-processing art has included different variations and methods of heating to prevent oxidation in green tea, varying temperatures and times for black tea oxidation, and attempting to make a jade oolong that matches my favorite imports from Taiwan or Fujian. The most important thing is to enjoy yourself as you go from garden to leaf to cup, savoring the sensory journey through the textures and aromas in processing your own tea.

## TEA AND FERMENTATION

Although classic black tea is oxidized and not fermented, Chinese pu'erh or "dark tea" is created from leaves allowed to ferment with various fungi and bacterial communities. These can occur naturally or be sprayed on to encourage the process. It's not hard to imagine the accidental discovery of fermented tea— perhaps a storage mistake in an especially humid environment! Pu'erh is an advanced technique and beyond the scope of this book. Temperature must be controlled or the tea may become more like compost—good for use in the garden, but probably not for drinking.

Kombucha is another popular fermented product traditionally made using tea. The SCOBY (Symbiotic Culture of Bacteria and Yeast) feeds on caffeine, tannins, and added sweeteners, creating a lightly carbonated, slightly acidic drink. Many people make this popular drink at home. We aren't aware of any commercial kombucha products using fresh or local tea (yet) but imagine this would enhance the drink's health appeal and benefits.

Several cultures use fresh tea leaves in a fermented form, such as the "pickled-leaf" lahpet, used in Burmese cooking. The strong bitter flavors of tea, especially when leaves are pickled, provide an excellent balance to the spicy flavors of traditional cuisines in this Southeast Asian region. As the methods for making lahpet seem rather simple, this is definitely one of my future culinary adventures!

Inspired by Moroccan mint tea, cold green tea steeps with fresh mint for a refreshing afternoon treat.

# Gardening with Tea

Plenty has been written about designing tea gardens, especially the traditional Japanese and Chinese types, as well as cottage gardens. Many gardening books have also been written about herbs used to make tisanes (non-camellia-based tea drinks). The term *tea garden* also sometimes refers to larger tea plantations, and has also been used to describe a social hangout (not unlike a coffee house). Historical English and American tea or pleasure gardens were popular places to take tea and mingle with diverse companions, enjoying various entertainments including walks, gazebos and private dining areas, dancing, and even fireworks.

Altogether, there is precedent for designing a variety of modern homegrown pleasure gardens where traditional tea plants play an important role but are part of a larger experience centered around enjoying tea in an outdoor setting. Whether your garden functions as a solitary, meditative space, a social venue, or both, is up to you. At present mine is both—my favorite place to enjoy drinking tea by myself (especially an iced tea on a hot summer afternoon) or with company is the shady grove overlooking my own plot of *Camellia sinensis*.

**AS A FLOWERING EVERGREEN,** tea has great potential for use in a variety of garden settings. A single plant can grow as a neatly trimmed centerpiece or can fill a large space, expanding as seedlings plant themselves underneath. Tea can also be planted as a delicious hedge. Well-trimmed tea can be a lovely addition to a formal garden, either as a border or demarcation in a larger garden, or along a wall or fence line. Though relatively slow-growing, a tea hedge will provide leaves for harvesting as well as flowers from late summer into early winter. Bees and other pollinators love tea flowers, so your tea hedge can make for beautiful and nourishing fall forage—sometimes you'll see multiple bees gathering on the bright yellow center of a single flower. Finally, as a legacy plant, tea can survive for decades in the landscape, providing pleasure and sustenance for future generations of humans and bees alike.

A feast for bees in fall, tea flowers support pollinators.

Just as camellia flowers have been selected for their diverse colors and forms, natural variation in *Camellia sinensis* has yielded notable and interesting varieties. For example, *C. sinensis* var. *sinensis* f. *rosea* has deep maroon-colored new growth with light pink flowers in fall. The dark leaves make a lovely contrast in a tea garden. Rosea tea (unrelated to "purple tea," developed and cultivated in Kenya) is impractical for commercial production due to small leaf size and slow growth. But we regularly harvest and process rosea leaf for personal consumption—it yields a delicious, subtly different flavor and slightly pink-tinged infusion.

The attractive cultivar *Camellia sinensis* var. *sinensis* f. *macrophylla* 'Yellow Tea' has large leaves with eye-catching variegated coloring. It grows slowly, so it works well as an ornamental specimen. Tea brewed from its leaves has been described as bitter, but we can't say from personal experience, since its slow growth has limited our making tea from it.

This tea flower is only just opening, but the bee doesn't want to wait.

Perhaps you are a collector of diverse plants, or maybe you simply want something unique for your garden. While tea is already different from most camellias you'll see in your neighborhood, other interesting cultivars include the variegated 'Silver Dust' and 'Gold Splash'. Compared with rosea and 'Yellow Tea', these are more similar in form to traditional small-leaf tea. We've made tea from them, and their taste is only subtly different.

**ABOVE** Intensely colored new growth of *C. sinensis* var. *sinensis* f. *rosea*.

**OPPOSITE, CLOCKWISE FROM TOP LEFT** Rosea's small leaves are no match for producing the same volume of tea as from the larger leaves of var. *assamica*, but their flavor is unique and delicious.

The large variegated leaves of 'Yellow Tea'.

The dappled foliage of 'Silver Dust' makes an interesting focal point in a garden.

The cultivar 'Gold Splash' has a subtly patterned leaf and produces a tea similar to traditional var. *sinensis*.

# Companion Planting for Pleasure

**PLANTING A TEA** garden offers abundant opportunities for creativity, with an endless array of colors, forms, and flavors available to delight the eye and palate. While traditional teas are delicious on their own, you can also cultivate a range of companion plants to create classic blends or try your hand at creative tea crafting. The ideas here are just a start, and of course the most suitable plants will vary by climate.

Bee balm (*Monarda didyma*) adds a splash of color to our garden and black tea blends at Camellia Forest.

## HERBS

If you have only a limited quantity of homegrown tea, blending is one good way to make it go further in the cup. Of all the herbaceous offerings, several favorites have particularly good potential for blending. One of the most popular is peppermint, which comes in many variants and makes a great combination with green tea. Other herbal candidates especially good for blending with green tea include lemongrass, lemon verbena, thyme, rosemary, and sage. I would never personally blend a strong-flavored herb with a first-flush green or white tea. But sometimes I find that adding herbs to teas made from leaf harvested in the high heat of summer (which to me seem more robust and less refined in flavor) makes for a lovely combination. Take a cautious approach to blending. Some herbs can be quite strong and easily overpower tea's subtle aromas—a little goes a long way.

On the other end of the spectrum, black tea is complemented by blending with bee balm, another member of the mint family. The flowers of *Monarda didyma* (red) or *Monarda fistulosa* (pink, lavender, or white) impart a citrus-like taste similar to Earl Grey, which is traditionally scented with fruit from *Citrus ×aurantium* subsp. *bergamia*. This bergamot orange tree grows in Mediterranean climates, and some gardeners (for example, on the west coast of California) may be able to grow both tea and oranges! Tea growers in Hawaii enjoy combining edible native flowers with their Hawaii-raised black tea to make a unique local product for locals to enjoy and tourists to take home.

Dried bee balm flowers impart a bergamot aroma to black tea, similar to Earl Grey.

## FLOWERS

Several years ago, I began researching flowers for blending with tea. Jasmine flowers appear in some of the best-known floral tea blends in Western countries. *Jasminum sambac*, the variety traditionally used for tea, is typically a tropical to subtropical plant. Other flowers used for scenting or blending with tea include the small, extremely fragrant flowers of *Osmanthus ×fortunei* or *Osmanthus fragrans*, gardenia flowers, rose petals, and blossoms from cherries and Japanese flowering apricot (*Prunus mume*). Inspired by a practice in Vietnam, in which a lotus blossom is filled with tea that absorbs the flower's scent, I've used summer-blooming magnolia flowers for their fragrance (though I don't recommend including the floral parts in your tea infusion, as they are very strong).

Flowers from the tea plant can also be delicately aromatic. To scent your tea, add fresh flowers to dried tea and cover for one to two

Rose petals can be used to scent many different kinds of tea, including green (as seen here), white, or even black.

days. The flower-to-tea ratio will vary based on amounts on hand, though, as with herbal blending, I suggest taking a conservative approach for strong-smelling blooms, which can overwhelm the tea's own aroma. After scenting, remove the flowers and redry the tea at a low temperature before storing it. Or, if your flowers are small, you can leave them to dry in the tea. Note that removing tea flowers in fall may support vegetative growth, but it will also prevent seeds from forming the next year, not to mention deprive pollinators of beneficial support.

These are simply a few ideas to get you started. Depending on where you live and what you grow, other opportunities may present themselves. JD Farms in Mississippi makes the most of their combined blueberry and tea farm, with a unique blend of green tea, jasmine flowers, hibiscus, and dried blueberries. Look around your garden or think about what you might like to grow—you'll find plenty of inspiration for delicious tea blends.

We love the contrast of black tea with white gardenias.

**CLOCKWISE FROM TOP LEFT**

An opening magnolia blossom reveals a delightful scent.

Now filled with black tea, the citrus-like aroma adds to the taste of an iced tea.

Used in a variety of Chinese foods, including tea, tiny osmanthus flowers yield powerful scent—a little goes a long way!

*Camellia sinensis* flowers have a faint scent that can complement a delicate white tea.

Fragrant blossoms from *Prunus mume*, Japanese flowering apricot, can be used to scent green tea.

# Working with What You Have

**ADDING TEA INTO** an existing garden is not as complicated as it might seem. Key considerations remain: drainage, sunlight, and protection from extremes. As we've established, good drainage is critical for growing tea, whether in pots or in the ground. After a heavy rain, watch your garden carefully to see where water pools and how long it takes before the soil begins to dry out. Soil often becomes compacted near the foundation of a home or driveway. Add soil conditioners like compost or PermaTill if you need them, and consider structural fixes like raised beds, ditches, and drains.

Observe where the sun shines throughout the day in all seasons, since this changes throughout the year. Look for a site with at least 50 percent sun during the growing season. In a hot climate, and especially in hot and dry climates, look for shade that falls in midday and late afternoon. Shade not only shelters your plants from excessive heat but it's also a more comfortable scenario for the people who tend them. If excess sun is a problem, companion shade plants may help. Alternatively, an arbor is an attractive option, and shade cloths, available at many home garden centers, provide flexibility in placement along with variable shapes and sizes to accommodate your particular situation. In a cold climate, look for morning shade and afternoon sun. In a climate like ours in North Carolina—cold in winter and hot in summer—a balance of both is nice.

# Tea Gardening for Health

**WE MAKE NO** health claims about homegrown versus bought tea, except for the following observation: not only is drinking tea a delicious and healthful alternative to sodas or energy drinks, *growing* tea also offers benefits to gardeners at a variety of ability and activity levels. Planting requires a bit of digging, some carrying, probably some bending and stooping—all of which gets you outside and moving. If you have a bad back or other limited mobility, you can get help with these more labor-intensive stages, then reap the physical health benefits of tending mature tea plants. Depending on how many plants you have, your arms and shoulders can get a bit of a workout with pruning and plucking. Keep your plants low enough to reduce strain if you plan to pluck a lot (this is a lesson vineyards had to learn, too, training their grapevines to grow at an easier height for the posture of cultivators). Last, but not least, time spent in the garden is a proven mental health and morale booster. Relish the peace and tranquility that comes while harvesting on a warm summer morning and the pleasure of knowing you'll soon enjoy a cup of your very own tea.

On a rainy afternoon, wandering through the tea garden provides a welcome break and reminder of all that is peaceful and beautiful in the world.

# More Fun with Tea

For many of us who gravitate toward creative ventures, tea experiments are immensely satisfying. Fortunately, there are a wealth of projects enterprising tea growers can spin off from their tea gardens. These range from simple crafting using harvest byproducts—as with roasted stem tea—to making shaded tea and matcha. Sometimes when my processed tea doesn't turn out as I'd hoped, I look for ways to use the leftover leaves. Growers in our survey reported using tea in many ways—these include adding tea to cosmetic products, such as soap and lotions, making tea-infused spirits, and cooking with tea. In this chapter, we highlight a few fun ideas, with a particular focus on fresh leaves, since there are plenty of other resources on using processed tea.

# Making Matcha

**BECAUSE TEA DRINKING** spread (along with Buddhist culture) to Korea and Japan at about the same time "whipped" tea was popular in China, this style became central to the tea culture in those countries. Centuries later, matcha remains a central feature of Japanese tea ceremonies and has spread to many cooking products. This green tea–based drink is now a trendy health food enjoyed by consumers around the world. Tea grown for the production of matcha is shaded in the two to three weeks before harvest, enriching the chlorophyll content and theanine levels, which contribute to the characteristic intense green, sweet flavor.

At Camellia Forest, we have experimented with making our own shaded tea using a simple structure of bamboo poles covered with multiple layers of shade cloth. Shade should be about 60–80 percent in the first couple weeks, and it can be increased to close to 90 percent in the week prior to harvest. On a row of tea that's already partially shaded by pine trees, we added three layers of 40 percent shade cloth, which is what we use on our greenhouses. At harvest time, leaves grown under the shade were a darker green (this color difference persisted through processing) and somewhat softer than leaves with

**CLOCKWISE, FROM BOTTOM LEFT**
Our bamboo and shade-cloth structure stood for three weeks.

Against a close-up of the shade cloth's texture, a shaded leaf (left) is noticeably darker than an unshaded leaf (right).

Traditional steeping isn't the only way to use your tea.

**ABOVE** Fresh green leaves are dried, but not rolled, before grinding into matcha powder.

**OPPOSITE** My quick and easy matcha.

more sun exposure. Our makeshift double-tent structure, an economical use of extra bamboo poles we had lying around, was tall enough to give the plants room to grow; however, any parts of the cloth touching new growth led to stunted leaves. If you plan to try this tent method, we recommend you design your structures carefully, making sure to account for wind, as they will need to endure whatever spring weather brings (we often have strong thunderstorms blow through). In cold climates, more sturdy structures might provide a frame for plastic sheeting over the shade cloth to temporarily protect the plants from extreme weather.

In processing tea for matcha, we followed the basic process for Japanese steamed tea, but with the shortest duration of steaming (fifteen seconds). After steaming, we didn't roll the leaves, but sent them directly into drying. Once dry, the tea is called *tencha* (to become matcha it must be ground into a fine powder). The stems should be removed before grinding. Modern factory techniques use electrostatic fanning to separate out these tougher pieces. At home, working with small amounts of leaf (and small leaves), this can be done by delicately rolling the dried leaves between your fingers to break them apart and carefully separating out the stems by hand. We purchased an affordable home grinder through the mail from Japan, which easily managed small amounts of leaf. Because powder granules have much more surface area compared with a whole leaf, fresh matcha can degrade quickly—we recommend storing the dried leaf intact and grinding it fresh just before using.

If you're pressed for time, but craving matcha, I have developed a shortcut to a very matcha-like green tea powder. All you have to do is microwave fresh leaves in thirty-second increments until dry and crispy. Remove stems and grind or pulverize to a powder just before use. Voilà, green, grassy goodness.

There are entire books dedicated to using matcha in a variety of ways, from the traditional whipped-tea method to using it to flavor food. Our personal favorite is including matcha powder when making fresh ice cream, going easy on the sugar to maximize the taste of the tea. But you don't have to restrict your matcha use to food. In addition to its antioxidant properties, green tea also has antibacterial properties, which makes it a natural addition to soaps and cosmetics, such as those made by Tulloch Tea in Scotland. Their founder, Lucy Williams, shared with us a simple recipe for making lip balm with homegrown matcha.

# Tulloch Tea's Matcha and Sweet Orange Lip Balm

**INGREDIENTS**

1 teaspoon sweet almond oil infused with matcha

3 teaspoons beeswax

3 teaspoons shea butter

1 teaspoon jojoba oil

8 drops sweet orange oil

20 drops vitamin E oil

**INSTRUCTIONS**

Melt beeswax, shea butter, and oils together in a bowl over a pan of boiling water.

Remove from heat and leave to cool slightly.

Add essential oil and vitamin E. Stir.

Pour directly into individual containers (small tins or glass pots).

Allow to solidify before using.

## MATCHA-INFUSED SWEET ALMOND OIL (MAKE AHEAD)

Stir 1 teaspoon fresh matcha powder into 4 ounces (¼ cup) sweet almond oil in an air-tight container. Stir or invert occasionally and before using. You may want to strain the oil through cheesecloth to remove large particles, especially if you haven't used a fine grind. Although it won't keep indefinitely, this infused oil can be kept for future batches or other recipes for healthful skincare.

# Cooking with Tea

**WHEN YOU FIRST** begin making your own tea, its small quantity will feel especially precious, and it can be difficult to conceive of throwing away the leaves after you've enjoyed your drink. Luckily, spent leaves can be enjoyed again in a variety of recipes. Some of my favorites include adding green tea leaves to stir-fry dishes and sprinkling black or oolong tea in rice while it cooks. Though important flavors and aromas come about during the process of drying, the adventurous cook may want to experiment with simply using steamed or stir-fried leaves.

Tea-boiled eggs are just one way tea can be incorporated into cooking—for recipe see next page.

# Tea-Boiled Eggs

When living in Taiwan, Susan learned to use processed tea to add flavor to many dishes. Rolling hardboiled eggs to crack their shells then boiling them further in strong tea is a traditional and attractive Chinese appetizer.

## INGREDIENTS

12 eggs

3 tablespoons black tea or 6 tablespoons or more used tea leaves

3 tablespoons soy sauce

2 tablespoons salt

1 tablespoon star anise seeds

## INSTRUCTIONS

Put eggs in cold, lightly salted water over medium flame; remove after 25 minutes when water is at a hard boil.

Place drained eggs in cold water for a few minutes to preserve the yolks' yellow color.

Crack eggs by rolling lightly on a hard surface or tapping all over with the back of a spoon.

Combine cracked eggs, tea, and other ingredients in a large saucepan and cover with water. Simmer for 1 hour.

Serve hot or cold. Shell eggs just before serving to admire the antique porcelain pattern. Good for several days in the refrigerator.

# Green Tea–Leaf Salad

Mix about 3 tablespoons freshly made green tea (preferably steamed), or leftovers from a 12-ounce pot of tea, with ½ teaspoon each of rice vinegar, soy sauce, and sesame oil (adjust to taste). Serve over one portion of rice and top with sesame seeds. This is tasty either cold or warm and is a great starting point for your own combinations.

# Tea-Infused Sugar or Salt

Tea-infused sugar or salt is a simple way to start cooking with your tea, and it has many uses. Use either the sugar or the salt in dry rubs or marinades. Try a tea-infused finishing salt for pork, fish, and poultry. Add the sugar infusion to garnish cookies, drink rims, or the crystalline bit on a crème brûlée—or make a simple syrup with 1 cup infused sugar to 1 cup water for use in cocktails. A combo of the sugar and salt is great for curing salmon.

### INSTRUCTIONS

Place 1 cup kosher salt or organic sugar (no powdered sugar) in an airtight container (use glass if possible).

Add fresh tea leaves (or leaves that have been withered or partially processed) into the sugar or salt and press gently to release the essences. For convenience, you can put the leaves in a small mesh bag first.

Cover with some more sugar or salt and mash everything together.

Close the lid and wait. Stir the sugar or salt every day until you get the flavor strength you desire—usually around one week.

Use a sifter to remove the leaves, or simply remove the mesh bag if you used one. Store your infusions in a plastic-lidded (I find metal lids begin to degrade with time, making plastic better for storage) and labeled mason jar. Add one of those silica packets that so often come with freeze-dried treats or seaweed to keep moisture at bay.

# Camellia-Poached Chicken

Boneless chicken breasts are poached to tender, juicy perfection in just minutes. Perfect with a light green salad and iced tea on a hot summer day.

## INGREDIENTS

2 boneless chicken breasts

1 teaspoon peppercorns

1 clove garlic

1 large onion, sliced

¼ cup fresh tea leaves

1 bay leaf

chicken broth

## INSTRUCTIONS

Place chicken, tea leaves, peppercorn, garlic, onion, and bay leaf in a shallow pan.

Pour in enough broth to cover chicken about halfway.

Bring to a boil, then reduce heat and simmer uncovered for five minutes.

Turn off heat, cover, and allow to rest for fifteen minutes.

Slice or shred chicken and reserve broth for use in recipes or to serve with chicken.

# Tempura Tea Leaves with Ponzu

Best suited to new growth and softer leaves (we actually liked the slightly larger new growth better than the tips). This treat has none of the bitterness of fresh leaf and makes a super enjoyable snack.

## INGREDIENTS

**A few handfuls of fresh tea leaves, washed or inspected and trimmed of any debris**

**3 cups vegetable, peanut, or tea seed oil**

**1 cup rice or all-purpose flour (Note: rice flour will result in a crispier product, with more leaf showing through)**

**1 tablespoon cornstarch**

**1 cup seltzer water**

**Sea salt**

**Ponzu sauce**

## INSTRUCTIONS

Heat oil in a small, deep pot to 375°F. You can test oil temperature by dropping a leaf in it. If bubbles start sizzling around the leaf, the oil is ready.

While you're waiting for the oil to heat, whisk together the flour, cornstarch, and seltzer water in a medium bowl.

Coat the leaves lightly in your batter.

Fry. You can fry about five leaves at a time depending on their size. When they get just golden, transfer to a plate lined with a paper towel. Sprinkle the hot tempura with a bit of sea salt and serve immediately with ponzu sauce.

## PONZU SAUCE (MAKE AHEAD)

### INGREDIENTS

**½ cup soy sauce**

**½ cup citrus juice (I love a mixture of 6 tablespoons Meyer lemon juice plus 2 tablespoons orange juice)**

**zest from one lemon**

**2 tablespoons mirin**

**dash of fish sauce**

### INSTRUCTIONS

Combine all the ingredients in a sterilized mason jar and mix well. Steep in the refrigerator overnight or up to a week.

A note on citrus juice: I prefer Meyer lemons when in season, but you can also experiment with a mixture of juices from lemon, orange, lime, yuzu, or grapefruit.

# White Tea–Infused Jellies

While technically not made with fresh green leaf, this recipe *can* be made with leaves that have gone through most of the process for making white tea but haven't fully dried.

## INGREDIENTS

3 ½ tablespoons of agar agar powder

3 teaspoons white leaf infused in 1 ½ cups filtered water

## INSTRUCTIONS

Let tea steep for at least six minutes. (Note: you may need more water depending on how dry your leaves are. Make a stronger tea infusion than you would normally like to drink— the sugar in the agar agar balances the astringency.)

Put tea (either strained or with the leaves left in for an interesting variation) and powder in a small saucepan and stir on high heat to dissolve crystals. As soon as the mixture starts to bubble, turn heat down to medium and stir for one minute. Remove from heat.

Don't leave the mixture sitting around too long because, unlike animal-based gelatin, agar agar gels quickly as it cools. Immediately pour into clean silicone molds or onto a sheet pan.

Once it has cooled to room temperature, the jelly should be firm. Pop gently out of molds or, if on a sheet pan, cut shapes with a knife or cookie cutters.

# OTHER CREATIVE USES FOR TEA

Tea can be used to impart flavor to cooking oils (similar to the matcha-infused sweet almond oil on page 182) and vinegars, as well as spirits and other alcoholic beverages. Published recipes mostly specify using processed tea, so adapting them to fresh leaf requires experimentation to determine whether raw leaves can transmit the desired flavor. One grower in our survey reports using tea to flavor bitters, which seems like a good fit.

**WRAPPING TEA LEAVES AROUND FOOD** during baking or smoking can add the tang of tea to a variety of foods. This is a great way to use any larger, older leaves left after pruning. A word of warning though: in an attempt to flavor some barbeque, I once added a batch of dried branches with leaves to the grill. I quickly discovered these are prone to burn and will scorch food. Fresh leaves or branches may be a better choice for high-temperature cooking.

**DYEING CLOTH WITH TEA** is an old practice, probably from the times when stains were difficult to remove. An overoxidized batch of black tea recently helped me rescue a few white napkins I found at a yard sale. I simply boiled the napkins in a pot with the leaves and they turned a lovely reddish brown. You might consider adding a little alum or cream of tartar to the water to set the color so it lasts longer. Some sources will advise you to avoid using modern laundry soaps to wash your tea-dyed items, as they are formulated to remove tannin stains. However, it's worth noting that nothing I've ever used in the laundry, including bleach, has been able to remove tea stains from the flour sack cloths I use for rolling tea leaves during processing—perhaps the juice from fresh leaves on a dry cloth is a more potent combination!

# Tea Gardens for Pleasure and Profit

**WE HIGHLY RECOMMEND** tea garden tourism. As avid tea gardeners and historians, Susan and I have enjoyed visiting other tea growers throughout the United States and abroad. Many growers invite visitors, and we encourage you to contact growers you may know of or those featured in our book if you want to learn more about them. If you have a specific type of tea you would like to emulate with your homegrown leaf, consider visiting the region where it comes from—whether it's Assam, Darjeeling, or Yunnan. Always keep in mind that technique is teachable, but terroir is unique.

Touring agricultural areas for entertainment is popular around the globe—think apple picking, pumpkin patches, and vineyard tours. Tea tourism is a natural outlet for growers and those organizations seeking to support them. Through its university extension service Small Farm Program, the University of California provides a very informative webpage and series of links about agritourism and specialty crops such as tea. The state of Hawaii's university-linked sites also provide encouragement for and information about tea

Even after the tea stops growing, an abundance of tea flowers is a treat for garden visitors in autumn.

tourism. Along with providing excellent how-to booklets produced by affiliated agronomists, the University of Hawaii runs a Japanese tea house at the East-West Center and a "Way of Tea Center" connected to its Japanese studies program. Many Hawaiian growers see tea cultivation within the context of their state's history, culture, and population. At Tea Hawaii and Company, Eva Lee and Chiu Leong provide tours of their attractively maintained grounds and tea-processing areas. The tours feature tastings, opportunities for native birdwatching, and information about their work on native tree preservation. Several other Hawaiian growers use similar features to attract customers and sell their local harvest. Tourist shops around the islands also serve as an outlet for tea grown in the state as a unique souvenir—lightweight, unbreakable, and easy to transport.

Tea growers from the southern United States to the Pacific Northwest, and from Cornwall to Scotland, also seek to share their work with tourists, as places to stop for refreshments, education, and gifts. Alabama tea grower Donnie Barrett has lured busloads of tourists sightseeing in neighboring Florida across the state line to visit his farm and sample his tea wares. He offers iced tea and light snacks, a field tour (weather permitting), and an entertaining, informative lecture. In North Carolina, at Camellia Forest, we offer a combination of free community-oriented events, tea education and processing workshops, and "pick your own" opportunities. At the opposite end of the climate range, the microplantation run by Lynne Collinson on Shapinsay, off the coast of Scotland, welcomes visitors to have a look around the still-developing site, which includes the large polytunnel where tea plants are propagated. And on the west coast of British Columbia, Westholme Tea Company has an on-site tea house and pottery shop where visitors can enjoy curated and homegrown offerings.

These days, thanks to high interest in local foods and artisan tea, there's an abundance of diverse opportunities for turning a tea hobby into income (we know of one grower who sets up a booth at local fairs for "tea-leaf fortune telling"), despite some of tea's unique challenges. Because tea is a slow-growing crop at first, growers have to make a substantial investment upfront before production can begin. While the economics of becoming a tea farmer are beyond the scope of this book, we predict that local tea stories will multiply in the coming years. Yours may become one of them, or you can support existing farmers by visiting and enjoying their products. Tea growers cultivate a friendly community of lifelong learners. We hope that you and your fellow beginning growers will find inspiration and join us on the journey.

# Resources and References

This chapter provides information for readers wanting to go further and learn more about tea history, production, and growth in the United States. We expect information and resources about growing tea to increase as awareness and practice of homegrown tea spreads.

## Where to Buy Tea Plants

We recommend, when possible, obtaining tea plants and seeds from local growers who have a history of tea cultivation in your region or know enough about the origins of their plants to be able to describe where they came from specifically and how you might expect them to perform in your individual growing situation. Although it's not always the case, online orders from anonymous sources may deliver mislabeled or lesser-quality products (especially seeds, which tend to dry out and lose viability with improper storage). The following is a list of providers we trust. It represents a range of geographical areas and providers based on availability at the time we are writing, but we're certain this list will grow. If possible, talk to other growers and keep up with the tea community. New providers and new, locally adapted plants will continue to appear.

- Camellia Forest Nursery: camforest.com
- Camellia Shop: camelliashop.com
- Minto Island Tea Company: mintoislandtea.com
- Nuccio's Nurseries: nucciosnurseries.com
- Tregothnan: tregothnan.co.uk

### GENERAL TEA-RELATED RESOURCES

- American Specialty Tea Alliance: specialtyteaalliance.org
- Cup and Leaf blog: cupandleaf.com
- US League of Tea Growers: usteagrowers.com

# Contributors

Here is a partial list of tea growers who contributed their stories for this book. Many allow tours or scheduled visits and all are part of the wonderful tea-growing community with much wisdom to impart.

Lori and Bob Baker, BLTeas at Heron's Meadow Farm, blteas.com

Donnie Barrett, Fairhope Tea Plantation, fairhopeteaplantation.com

Lynne Collinson, Orkney Island Tea, lynncollinson3@gmail.com

Donald Fraser, Guisachan, friendsofguisachan.org

Eliah Halpenny and Cam Muir, Big Island Tea, bigislandtea.com

Mike Hyatt, Isle of Lismore Tea, @Baleveolancroft on Facebook

Eva Lee, Tea Hawaii and Company, teahawaii.com

Angela McDonald, Labrang Tea Traders, lmftea.com

Jason McDonald, Great Mississippi Tea Company, greatmsteacompany.com

Elizabeth Miller, Minto Island Tea Company, mintoislandtea.com

Joanna Ramos, Virginia First Tea Farm, virginiafirstteafarm.com

Don Vanderwerken, JD Farms and Pearl River Tea, jdfarms.us

Beverly Wainwright, Tea Gardens of Scotland, teagardensofscotland.co.uk

Lucy Williams, Tulloch Tea, @tullochtea on Facebook and Instagram

# Online Resources

Several universities have produced and posted guides for tea growers on a variety of subjects from agritourism to soil conditions, including the University of California, Davis, and the University of Hawaii's College of Tropical Agriculture and Human Resources. A targeted search at the website ctahr.hawaii.edu using the word "tea" provides numerous research-based reports. For its members, the United States League of Tea Growers provides a variety of materials on its website, including a brief beginner's guide to plant sources and global tea cultivation. The American Specialty Tea Alliance also provides a variety of tea-education resources.

Methods of testing and adjusting soil pH are available on the websites of Oregon State University and the Royal Horticultural Society (RHS). In the United States, the National Centers for Environmental Information maintain a website (ncdc.noaa.gov) with information on temperature, humidity, and rainfall ranges, as well as (ugh) pests. For the United Kingdom, web-based information sources include videos and information from specific tea sources such as the Tea Gardens of Scotland and the gardens of Tregothnan in Cornwall.

# References

Ackerman, William L. *Beyond the Camellia Belt*. Chicago: Ball Publishing, 2007.

Burgess, Anthony (preface). *The Book of Tea*. Paris: Flammarion, 1992.

Chang, Hung Ta, and Bruce Bartholomew. *Camellias*. Portland: Timber Press, 1984.

Chen, Liang, Zeno Apostolides, and Zong-Mao Chen (eds.). *Global Tea Breeding*. New York: Springer, 2012.

Danying, Guo, and Wang Jianrong. *The Illustrated Book of Chinese Tea*. Hangzhou: Zhejiang Photographic Press, 2013.

Fuchs, Jeff. *The Ancient Tea Horse Road*. Ontario: Penguin Group Canada, 2008.

Gascoyne, Kevin, Francois Marchand, Jasmin Desharnais (eds.). *Tea: History, Terroirs, Varieties*. Buffalo: Firefly Books, 2011.

Hajra, N. Ghosh. *Tea Cultivation Comprehensive Treatise*. Lucknow: International Book Distributing Company, 2001.

Harney, Michael. *The Harney and Sons Guide to Tea*. New York: Penguin, 2008.

Heiss, Mary Lou, and Robert J Heiss. *The Tea Enthusiast's Handbook: A Guide to Enjoying the World's Best Teas*. Berkeley: Ten Speed Press, 2010.

Hoyt, Scott Chamberlin, and Phil Cousineau. *The Meaning of Tea: A Tea Inspired Journey*. New York: Talking Leaves Press, 2009.

Jiyin, Gao, and Clifford R. Parks. *Collected species of the Genus Camellia an Illustrated Outline*. Hangzhou: Zhejiang Science and Technology Publishing House, 2005.

Parks, Clifford R., and G. Y. Leung. "An analysis of three germination treatments on five camellia species." *American Camellia Society Yearbook*. 2010.

Pettigrew, Jane. *Jane Pettigrew's World of Tea*. Birmingham: 83Press, 2018.

Pettigrew, Jane, and Bruce Richardson. *A Social History of Tea: Tea's Influence on Commerce, Culture and Community*. Danville: Benjamin Press, 2013.

Pratt, James Norwood. *New Tea Lover's Treasury: The Classic True Story of Tea*. San Francisco: Tea Society, 1999.

Rose, Sarah. *For All the Tea in China: How England Stole the World's Favorite Drink and Changed History*. New York: Viking Penguin, 2010.

Smith, Junius. *Essays on the cultivation of the tea plant*. New York: W. E. Dean, 1848.

Trehane, Jennifer. *Camellias: The Gardener's Encyclopedia*. Portland: Timber Press, 2007.

Willson, K. C., and M. N. Clifford (eds.). *Tea: Cultivation to Consumption*. New York: Springer Science, 1992.

Zee, Francis, Dwight Sato, Lisa Keith, Peter Follett, and Randall T. Hamasaki. "Small-scale Tea Growing and Processing in Hawaii." College of Tropical Agriculture and Human Resources, University of Hawaii at Manoa, Cooperative Extension Service. 2003.

Zhen, Yong-su. *Tea: Bioactivity and Therapeutic Potential*. London: Taylor and Francis, 2002.

# Acknowledgments

This book reflects the inspiration, support, and shared experience of many people. My husband, David, is my partner in growing tea. I thank him for introducing me to the world of camellias, tea included. Many thanks also to my kids, who have grown up helping out at Camellia Forest, and to family and friends who have come to appreciate my fascination with tea. Thanks to Kate Erle, for her support and sharing her many talents, including designing realistic figures of pruning and frame formation. I'm also grateful to the interns and volunteers whose hard work make the tea garden flourish and who have shared their experiences, inspiration, and questions. And to the many fellow tea growers who helped along the way with feedback on chapters and various topics, I look forward to learning together in the years to come.  —Christine

My thanks extend to the over-100 growers who responded to our questionnaire, those who sent in information and photos, and many others who kindly spent time with us in their fields, sharing their experiences and samples of their home brews. Particular thanks go to my patient husband, who supported my tea travels and took terrific photos, some of which are included. Important insights also came from conversations with experts such as James Norwood Pratt, former Lipton tea consultant and site investigator John Vendeland, US tea pioneer and grower trainer at the University of Hawaii Francis Zee, and others whose love of tea continues to inspire.  —Susan

# Photo and Illustration Credits

Illustrations on pages 28, 89, 102, and 143 created by Kate Erle.

Unless listed, photos are by Christine Parks.

Milli Apelgren, pages 60, 61, 99 top, 128 bottom

Madelaine Au, page 123 left

Kate Earl, page 169 top

Donald Fraser, page 40

Kathy Hampton, pages 2, 6, 56–57, 68, 70 right, 76, 77 bottom right, 80, 93, 107, 153, 154, 167, 169 bottom, 175 top right, 179 bottom right

Mike Hyatt, page 41

Jason McDonald, The Great Mississippi Tea Company, page 29

Cam Muir, pages 125, 126–127, 128 top

Michael Pratt, page 121, 123 right

Joanna Kil Ramos, page 31

Victor Vesely, pages 32, 131

J. Andrew Walcott, pages 10, 11, 27, 34 bottom, 35 bottom, 37, 95 bottom, 101, 123 left, 135

Susan Walcott, page 35 top

Lucy Williams, page 132

**Public Domain**

Fortune, Robert. *Two visits to the tea countries of China and the British tea plantations in the Himalaya*. Volume 2, page 171. Biodiversity Heritage Library, page 20

Sarony & Major, lithographer. *The destruction of tea at Boston Harbor / lith. & pub. By Sarony & Major, 99 Nassau near i.e., near Fulton St., N.Y.* Boston Massachusetts United States, ca. 1846 [New York: Lith. & pub. By Sarony & Major, 99 Nassau near sic Fulton St., October 1]. Library of Congress, page 23

Wilson, Ernest Henry, photographer. Men laden with tea. Harvard, Arnold Arboretum Horticultural Library, page 19

Zhangzhugang. Creative Commons Attribution-Share Alike 3.0 Unported, Wikimedia Commons, page 21

**iStock**
Twomeows_IS, page 183

**Alamy**
StockphotoVideo / Alamy Stock Photo, page 163

# Index

World War II, 38
worm compost, 92, 99, 120. *See also* compost

## Y
yellowing of leaves, 111
yellow tea, 15, 123, 166
'Yellow Tea' cultivar, 169, 170
yellow tea mites, 113
Yunnan Province (China), 14, 18, 28, 46

## Z
Zee, Francis, 36
Zhu Ye Qing (Green Bamboo tea), 15

**CHRISTINE PARKS** is an environmental health scientist, avid gardener, and tea lover. Together with her husband, David, she developed Camellia Forest Tea Gardens in Chapel Hill, North Carolina, as a site to trial and curate their diverse collection of *Camellia sinensis* varieties, grow and produce tea, and provide an educational setting for nursery customers and visitors. The Parks family has worked for decades collecting, propagating, and testing camellia cultivars for hardiness—today Christine and David are partners in Tea Flower Research, which has formalized the family's work. She was chair of the Tea Committee of the American Camellia Society, and a founding member of the US League of Tea Growers and representative for southeastern growers. Christine gives tours and workshops onsite at Camellia Forest and classes and talks at various local, regional, and national venues.

**SUSAN M. WALCOTT** is an emerita professor of geography at the University of North Carolina at Greensboro. Her Scottish paternal grandparents were quite fond of their brisk brew of tea. Curiosity about a cup of South Carolina's American Classic tea on a quiet Friday led her to Wadmalaw Island, then several sojourns to the Hawaiian Islands. She has sipped soup-like buttery tea in Tibet and visited Hangzhou's tea gardens and tea museum during a research trip to China's high-technology parks—a geographers' curiosity leads down many roads. She is a founding member of the US League of Tea Growers, presents talks on tea with Christine, and has published several articles in academic journals on tea grown in the United States.